Reading the Gospel of John through Palestinian Eyes

Langham

PREACHING RESOURCES

As the skilled New Testament scholar that he is, Yohanna Katanacho does not insist that perspective is everything. Yet he does suggest that perspective matters a lot, and that as a Palestinian Christian citizen of Israel he reads a text like John's gospel best when he reads it with clarity regarding his own identity and context. The result is a delightful and moving take on the fourth gospel that manages to touch matters of identity, salvation, justice, and peace with a pen that moves both soberly and irenically. Palestinian Christians are painfully well placed to teach the rest of us how to speak truth in love. Katanacho does so here in an accessible volume that belongs on the shelf of every reader of English who cares about the Gospel of John.

David A. Baer, PhD
Director, Theological Education Initiative
Professor, Old Testament & Biblical Languages,
Seminario Bíblico de Colombia, Medellín, Colombia

Dr Yohanna Katanacho's insightful and accessible commentary on the Gospel of John is a feast of rich theological insight into the apostle's message for his day and our own. A faithful and careful interpreter of the biblical text, Katanacho reads John's story against the backdrop of the apostle's own time and within the setting of the contemporary Palestinian-Israeli conflict. This is biblical interpretation done from the road where life is tensely lived and not from the balcony. Reading along ancient and contemporary grains, Yohanna Katanacho offers Christians everywhere a fresh vision of the Fourth Gospel's universal message of hope and reconciliation in the one vine, who is Christ Jesus.

Gene L. Green, PhD
Professor Emeritus of New Testament,
Wheaton College and Graduate School, Wheaton, Illinois, USA

This book is a reflection on the Gospel of John that is rooted in the Word and relevant to the contemporary world. The insights are profound, provocative, and prophetic! This book deepens our understanding of our identity in Christ and how we, as his followers, ought to embody his love and justice in this world.

Theresa Roco-Lua, EdD
General Secretary, Asia Theological Association

To the sarcastic question, "Can anything good come out of Nazareth?" (John 1:46), I answer: "Yes, a book on biblical interpretation!" Yohanna Katanacho, a Palestinian Christian, helpfully reminds us that we all read the Bible through perspectives influenced by our respective places and times. Yet *Reading the Gospel of John through Palestinian Eyes* is not a paean to postmodernism, nor does it bow the knee to relativistic pluralism. Rather, Katanacho's reading is his humble and reasonable offering that both derives from and enriches the whole church, a distinct testimony – that of a Palestinian Christian citizen of Israel – to the Jewish Messiah who is Lord and Savior of every tribe and nation.

Kevin J. Vanhoozer, PhD
Research Professor of Systematic Theology,
Trinity Evangelical Divinity School, Deerfield, Illinois, USA

Reading the Gospel of John through Palestinian Eyes

Yohanna Katanacho

Langham

PREACHING RESOURCES

© 2020 Yohanna Katanacho

Published 2020 by Langham Preaching Resources
An imprint of Langham Publishing

www.langhampublishing.org

Langham Publishing and its imprints are a ministry of Langham Partnership

Langham Partnership
PO Box 296, Carlisle, Cumbria, CA3 9WZ, UK
www.langham.org

ISBNs:
978-1-78368-780-0 Print
978-1-78368-793-0 ePub
978-1-78368-794-7 Mobi
978-1-78368-795-4 PDF

Scriptures taken from the Holy Bible, New International Version®, NIV®. Copyright © 1973, 1978, 1984, 2011 by Biblica, Inc.™ Used by permission of Zondervan.

British Library Cataloguing-in-Publication Data
A catalogue record for this book is available from the British Library

ISBN: 978-1-78368-780-0

Cover & Book Design: projectluz.com

To the faculty of Trinity International University who shaped my life and taught me to love God with all of my heart and mind, with special gratitude to Drs Willem VanGemeren, Richard Averbeck, D. A. Carson, Kevin Vanhoozer, John Feinberg, the late Grant Osborne, and John Woodbridge.

I also dedicate this book to the amazing ministries of Langham Partnership and Scholar Leaders International. I am eternally thankful for their support and sacrificial love.

CONTENTS

Acknowledgements

I would like to express my special thanks and gratitude to Dr David Baer who examined the whole manuscript and provided many helpful suggestions. Special thanks to my colleague Mr Pierre Tannous who helped me in complex formatting issues. Dr Philip Sumpter graciously provided an in-depth theological discussion that shaped my thoughts. Dr Ron Fay, who is an expert on the Gospel of John, introduced me to important resources. Ms Beverley Timgren graciously edited the whole manuscript. Ms Janet Mikhail provided a second editorial opinion that helped me to smooth out the rough edges. The English professor Dr Evelyn Reynolds provided very helpful input.

I have taught the Gospel of John for more than twenty years. There is no doubt that most of my ideas have been shaped by my students at Bethlehem Bible College and Nazareth Evangelical College. These bright and godly students have challenged me to be more accurate and more contextual. Thank you.

I cannot thank my wife and boys enough. My wife Dina and my children, Immanuel, Jonathan and Christopher, allowed me to spend endless hours reading, praying, and studying the word of God. Their sacrifice made it possible for me to write this book. I am eternally thankful for their love and support. Last, but definitely not least, I thank God for empowering me to finish this book. *Soli Deo Gloria!*

Introduction

All of us read the Gospel of John from a particular perspective. Let us imagine that this perspective is a mental lens that we use in order to look at the text. For example, when we look at our hands, we see specific things such as our skin or perhaps some dirt, but, with a microscope, we see things that were invisible to the naked eye. In fact, the more lenses we use, the more perspectives we encounter. If we use yellow lenses or red lenses, what we see looks different because we see different colors. If we use a magnifying glass or a glass that reduces size, then the size of the text is not the same. Put differently, certain perspectives exaggerate particular features while others minimize specific traits.

People have been studying the Gospel of John for almost two thousand years. It is not my goal to address the numerous publications in the twentieth century, let alone throughout history.[1] But we must ask ourselves some important questions: What is the lens that we use when we look at the text? What are the factors that shape our mental lenses? Do we have a Christian or a Muslim or a Jewish lens when we look at the text? Is our lens Catholic, Baptist, Coptic, Presbyterian, Lutheran, Pentecostal, or Greek Orthodox? Obviously, the lenses about which I am talking are part of our mindset and are the factors that shape the way in which we look at things. In short, our perspectives are shaped by our social, political, educational, and religious locations.

It is unwise, therefore, to claim that our interpretations have no assumptions. They are not neutral or unbiased. Some in Israel/Palestine claim that their interpretation is "biblical." They usually use an Arabic equivalent (*Ktaby*) that literally means "scriptural." Such people argue that theirs is the correct or divine interpretation of the Bible, the interpretation that every believer would discover if he or she sincerely searched for it. This approach ignores the role of the interpreter and his or her biases. Consequently, the so-called "scriptural" interpretation might become an abusive tool in the hands of some dominant churches, some leaders, or a particular school of thought.

---

1. For details about recent research on the Gospel of John, please see the following: Pack, "Gospel of John in the Twentieth Century"; Songer, "Gospel of John in Recent Research"; Kysar, "Gospel of John in Current Research"; Stibbe, *Gospel of John as Literature*; Porter and Fay, *Gospel of John in Modern Interpretations*. See also Elowsky, *Commentary on the Gospel*, and Elowsky, *Commentary on John*, 2 vols.

Usually, this approach ignores different translations of the Bible, different manuscript traditions, the history of interpretation, diverse interpretations, hermeneutical developments, social sciences, and archaeology. The interpreter replaces God in claiming absolute truth and affirms: "Thus says the Lord." Thus, whoever disagrees with his or her scriptural interpretation opposes God. I don't mind using the Arabic expression "scriptural" (*Ktaby*) as long as we confess that our interpretations are open to criticism and correction.[2] Wise interpreters don't ignore the history of scholarship of a particular book or text. On the contrary, we, being sinful, must humble ourselves and adorn ourselves with the virtues of the kingdom of God as we seek divine truth. To say that our interpretations are 100 percent accurate, without allowing for possible faults in our perceptions, is problematic. It is arrogant and not compatible with a theology of humility. On the other hand, it is wise to affirm that our backgrounds and sociopolitical and cultural locations influence the way we think; even better, in fact, to state that our assumptions shape the way we perceive. With this affirmation we become humble and better listeners as we travel along the path in search of the truth.

In short, the same text could have several interpretations: Zionist, Catholic or Protestant. Some interpretive lenses draw us closer to divine truth while others drive us farther afield. But God is the judge who fully discerns what is true from what is false. Only God, the ultimate standard, is 100 percent true. As for human beings, time plays an important role in guiding us as we seek to distinguish right from wrong and differentiate between eternal and ephemeral wisdom. Time helps us to test our perspectives and discover whether they bring forth a blessing or a curse. Furthermore, Christ is the interpretive compass that guides us to a better understanding of Scripture. The universal church throughout the ages is a wise guide for all those who search for truth.

From the aforementioned interpretive perspective, and from a mindset that resists pride and does not look down on other points of view, I would like to present a Palestinian Israeli Christian reading of the Gospel of John. At the same time, I acknowledge that there are several Palestinian Christian views and that I don't represent all of them.[3] However, it is fair to say that most contemporary Palestinian Christian perspectives, if not all, have been

2. The Arabic word *Kitab* (كتاب) usually means a book. The word (*Ktaby*) in many Christian circles denotes not only what is in the Holy Bible but also what is normative. All Arabic transliteration generated by "Arabic to Latin Converter," MyLanguages.Org, 2019, http://mylanguages.org/arabic_romanization.php.

3. For a survey of some Palestinian perspectives, see Katanacho, "Palestinian Protestant Theological Responses."

shaped by similar sociopolitical and religious events, for we live in the context of occupation, discrimination, denominationalism, religious extremism, Judaization, Islamization, wars, hatred, and a tribal patriarchal society. For Palestinian Christians, our questions have been born and grown to what they are in this context. We have specific sociopolitical questions that have shaped the way in which we study the word of God and the kind of answers we seek. This is true for me as well.

I read Scriptures, including the Gospel of John, as a Palestinian who holds Israeli citizenship. I don't claim that my Palestinian reading or culture is superior or sinless (God alone is sinless). Yet, beginning with my identity as I have described it, I approach a text seeking the will of God and desiring to obey it. I read the Scriptures through a Palestinian cultural lens, and I read them as a Christian who lives within a Jewish majority, a fact that distinguishes my reading from other Arab Christians in other parts of the world.[4] It is also important to assert that my Palestinian identity is not a sin but a blessing and a bridge that needs to be sanctified in Christ. It enhances other readings and leads to the enrichment of the diverse perspective of the universal multicultural church. My reading challenges those that overlook the centrality of Christ and abuse the text in order to spread a view that empowers the oppressor rather than the oppressed. It challenges ethnocentric and nationalist perspectives and interpretations that are not interested in empowering every repentant person regardless of his or her cultural background.

Among the mindsets that I encounter in my context, some Messianic Jews believe that Jewish culture is indispensable for a proper understanding of the Gospel of John. Though the perspectives of Messianic Jews are diverse, and some accept the dominant ecclesiastical interpretations of the ages, most feel uncomfortable with Hellenistic culture and its language, which dominated church history.[5] Consequently, it is not uncommon to hear Messianic Jews challenging – or even refusing the use of – expressions like "Christ," "church," or "Trinity." They usually affirm the doctrinal realities behind these expressions, but they feel uncomfortable using "Hellenistic" expressions. Such proponents highlight the importance of Jewish culture and claim it as a foundation for understanding the text (an approach that presents serious problems in seeking common doctrinal grounds).[6]

---

4. I read the Arabic text and also consult the Greek text, as well as other languages, in order to verify my readings.

5. Further details about Messianic Jews can be found in Harvey, *Mapping Messianic Jewish Theology*, 96–139.

6. See, for example, Lizorkin-Eyzenberg, *Jewish Gospel of John*.

But these claims are not accurate when speaking of Jewish culture in the singular, as there exists in fact a spectrum of Jewish cultures and perspectives. For example, there is the Judaism of the Pharisees, the Essenes, and the Sadducees, as well as other forms of Judaism in the first century, to say nothing of many diverse embodiments of Judaism throughout the ages. Furthermore, each of these is perceived in different ways by its adherents and its opponents. In addition, it is not accurate to equate Judaism with the Old Testament. Rabbinic Judaism, for example, is not centralized around the priesthood, temple, and sacrifices. Also, some don't distinguish between the Jewishness of Jesus and the Jewishness of the members of the modern state of Israel. Thus, they turn the Jewishness of the Messiah into an identity that pushes away Palestinians and Arabs. His Jewishness, then, becomes a dividing wall that discriminates between his Jewish and his Greek followers. This approach fails to understand the theological meaning of Jewishness because it overlooks the fact that the Jewishness of Jesus is sinless, with no addition of selfishness, bigotry, or even ethnic exclusivism. Such an approach ignores the uniqueness of the Jewishness of Jesus that alone embodies the dreams of the Old Testament, calling all nations to worship the one true God. It paves the way for a new age; the prophets of the Old Testament hoped for a day in which the law would be internalized in the hearts of all peoples. Their dreams reached beyond ethnic Jewishness to eschatological covenantal Jewishness, namely, the hope and transformative worldview associated with the coming of the kingdom of God. In the latter, not only is the law internalized but also those who were considered strangers are able to become equal members in the family of God.

In addition to Messianic Jews, another Jewish group reads the Gospel of John in Israel, but they feel uncomfortable with its claims. For example, Adele Reinhartz is concerned because the Jesus of the Gospel of John describes first-century Jews as an unbelieving satanic seed (John 8:44), as well as being blind, sinners, and unable to understand their own Scriptures.[7] No wonder that some Israeli Jews are not interested in Jesus at all. In fact, some call him *Yeshu* (ישו) which has a different meaning from *Yeshua* (ישוע). *Yeshu* is a disputed expression. Some argue that it is a Hebrew acronym for a sentence that reads, "May God obliterate his name and memory!"[8] Jews in Israel use *Yeshu* even in public spaces, including TV broadcasting, newspapers, and museums.

---

7. Reinhartz, "Nice Jewish Girl," 179. See also Reinhartz, *Befriending the Beloved Disciple*.

8. The Hebrew text is ימח שמו וזכרו. It is transliterated as *ymh shmw wzkhrw*. The literal translation is "Let his name and memory be obliterated." See Kai Kjaer-Hansen, "An Introduction to the Names Yehoshua/Joshua, Yeshua, Jesus and Yeshu." JewsforJesus.org (1992); available

On the other hand, some Palestinians affirm that there is a sociocultural, geopolitical, and psychological continuum between the different oppressed peoples who have inhabited Palestine throughout the ages.[9] From this perspective, this unique connection includes modern Palestinians and makes Jesus a Palestinian. It is important to note that the term "Palestinian," used before 1948, included Jews who lived in Palestine, and Jesus was part of the same geography, culture, and geopolitical and psychological realities as other residents of Palestine. Palestinians continue the argument, saying that the identity and works of Jesus represent and embody the hopes of the Palestinian people more than other nations.

In addition, many Muslims see Jesus as a Muslim and a Palestinian prophet. They add that the Gospel of John includes prophecies about the coming of Muhammad, arguing that the referent of the Greek word *Paraclete* is Muhammad, not the Holy Spirit.[10] Furthermore, some Palestinian Christians affirm that Jesus Christ is the Son of God who was born in the Palestinian town of Bethlehem, while Palestinian liberation theologians claim that the Palestinian Jesus is facing Herod again. This time, his encounter is through the struggle of his church with the Israeli occupation.[11] In other words, we have made Jesus part of the problem instead of seeing him as part of the solution; we have overstated our arguments as we affirmed the Jewish or Palestinian identity of Jesus. No doubt, the identity of Jesus, his deeds, and his teachings are important to all of us. The better we understand these things, the more we understand God's plan for humanity. By presenting Jesus from a Palestinian Israeli evangelical perspective, it is my hope that this perspective will help us to discover our Lord Jesus Christ and to find our identity in him instead of conforming him to our identity. Furthermore, I hope that my study will contribute to a better understanding of the Gospel of John within the global church and also empower Palestinian contextual theologians as they reflect on Jesus Christ.

---

from https://jewsforjesus.org/answers/an-introduction-to-the-names-yehoshua/joshua-yeshua-jesus-and-yeshu/.

9. Raheb, "Toward a Hermeneutics of Liberation," 11–27; Raheb, *Faith in the Face of Empire.*

10. The common translation of *Paraclete* is comforter. For further discussion, see the following Arabic books: El Sakka, (السقا), بيركليت [Berkelet], 24–68; Abdel Salam (عبد السلام), محمد [The Gospel of John in scales]; في إنجيل يوحنا [Muhammad in the Gospel of John], 69–99; Zahran (زهران), إنجيل يوحنا في الميزان [The Gospel of John in scales]; Yakan (يكن), محمد رسول الله [Muhammad is the messenger of God].

11. Khoury (خوري), من أجل حدود مفتوحة بين الزمن والأبدية: نحو لاهوت متجسد [For an open border between time and eternity: Towards incarnational theology], 455. See also Ateek, *Palestinian Christian*; Raheb, *I Am a Palestinian Christian*; Katanacho, "Palestinian Protestant Theological Responses."

It is fitting, now, to explain my statement that we Palestinians and Messianic Jews have made Jesus part of the struggle instead of making him part of the solution. Many of our leaders have tried to make Jesus a "Jew" or a "Palestinian" in order to make political or ideological gains. Consequently, we have not paid enough attention to the identity of Jesus as declared in the ecumenical councils, especially in Chalcedon in AD 451.[12] The council known by that name declared that Jesus is fully God and fully human. He is 100 percent God and 100 percent human. The Father and the Son have the same divine essence. What is more, Jesus Christ has the same human essence as the rest of humanity. The fully eternal one, God the Son, was born of the Father before all ages. The fully human one, God incarnate, was born of the Virgin Mary, the mother of God.[13] He has two natures without mixture or transformation or division or separation. Each nature preserves all of its characteristics in one person that cannot be divided into two persons. This is the Chalcedonian Christ who represents all of humanity regardless of ethnic background.[14]

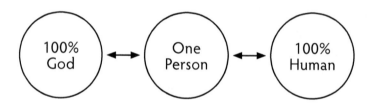

As an aside, it is true that Oriental Orthodox Christians (Copts, Syrian Orthodox, Ethiopian, Armenian Orthodox, and others) did not accept the Chalcedonian Creed. They do believe that Jesus Christ is fully God and fully human, and that he is one person, but they refuse to accept the phrase "two natures." They argue that it is not accurate to call them Monophysites, a term that is related to a heresy that accepted the divinity of Christ but rejected his humanity. They prefer the expression Miaphysites, meaning that the one nature of Christ is fully human and fully God without mixture, change, division, or separation.

---

12. Lorimer (لوريمر), تاريخ الكنيسة [Church history], 228–229.

13. For further information about the role and place of the Virgin Mary, especially the meaning of *Theotokos*, see Katanacho, and Katanacho (كتناشو و كتناشو), أطلقوني [Free me], 43–53.

14. Nestlehutt, "Chalcedonian Christology"; Moulder, "Is a Chalcedonian Christology Coherent?"; Young, "Council of Chalcedon."

It seems that Chalcedonian and non-Chalcedonian Christians agree in principle, even though they disagree about terminology.[15] Yet many, regardless of their denomination, are far from the Chalcedonian Christ. Ignoring the fact that Christ is fully human, and that his humanity represents people of all nations, including both Palestinians and Jews, they instead present an exclusive Christ. Thus, the Chalcedonian definition of Jesus is indispensable for a better understanding of the identity of Jesus Christ.

Nevertheless, the Chalcedonian definition does not address the relationship between the inclusive humanity of Jesus and his particular ethnicity. It does not address how Jesus can be a peacemaker, not only between humanity and God, but also between Jews and non-Jewish nations. In other words, Chalcedon does not clarify the meaning of the Jewishness of Jesus.

Therefore, I believe that we need to consider the identity of Jesus in new ways. Without doubt, the Gospel of John can enrich our understanding of valuable traditions related to the person of Jesus Christ, his life, and deeds. In light of the above, I suggest reading the Fourth Gospel in light of the following concerns: How can the Jewish Jesus, who was born in Palestine, and who is fully human, be our peacemaker and liberator? How can he represent both Palestinians and Jews as the humble servant who suffered, died, and rose from the dead? How can the Gospel of John reveal the full humanity of Christ in the context of the Palestinian-Israeli conflict and in an age in which humanity is distorted? The Gospel of John provides a promising theological space for such reflections.[16]

Put differently, those who understand the identity of Jesus in exclusive, national, and ethnic ways are advocating a political depiction of Jesus that is contrary to the inclusive Christ promoted in the Gospel of John. John challenges exclusive Pharisaic Judaism by rereading its major components in light of the inclusive Christ. I am not interested in reconstructing Pharisaic Judaism from an historical point of view, but in following its Johannine representation.[17] John is responding to a form of exclusive Judaism which I shall call Pharisaic Judaism. My interest is in John's response and the way he rereads his perceptions in light of the coming of Christ. Indeed, John examines

---

15. In 1984, the former Syrian Orthodox patriarch, Mar Ignatius Zakka I Iwas, issued a common declaration with Pope John Paul II. See "Common Declaration of Pope John Paul II and Hh Mar Ignatius Zakka I Iwas," Centre Pro Unione, Franciscan Friars of the Atonement, 23 June 1984, http://www.prounione.urbe.it/dia-int/oo-rc_syrindia/doc/i_oo-rc_syrindia_1984.html.

16. Katanacho, "Reading the Gospel."

17. For further information about Pharisaic Judaism, see Neusner, *From Politics to Piety*.

the relationship of Jesus to Jacob (4:12), to Moses (6:12; 9:28), and to Abraham (8:53). He examines how Jesus and his followers relate to the traditions of cleansing (2:1–11), holy space (2:18–22; 4:20–24), and holy time. He explains that Jesus works on the Sabbath (5:16; 9:16). He also examines the relationship of Jesus with the holy calendar, especially as it relates to Moses (6:1–8:29). He understands the holy Abrahamic community (8:30–59) and the holy land (10:1–21) in light of the coming of Christ. Thus, John presents a new world order that starts with the "enhumanization" of the second person of the Trinity and is completed with his death and resurrection. Enhumanization entails both enfleshment and ensoulment. It is etymologically a better rendering than incarnation, that is, enfleshment. Jesus became fully human, or following in the footsteps of the Nicene Creed, enhumanized.[18] In the folds of this new world order, we discover the importance of the centrality of the inclusive Christ.

I shall discuss in the following sections components of the "new beginning" that is presented in the Gospel of John: holy space, holy time, holy history, holy community, holy land, and a new perception of the meaning of life. These components are not only important in the Gospel of John but are also important for a theological reflection today. It is helpful to reflect on the meaning of the Old Testament from the perspective of John, and it is also empowering in the battle against ethnocentric exclusive theologies. The Gospel of John introduces christological Jewishness that is centered on the inclusive identity and works of Jesus Christ. Let us now look at the big picture of the Gospel of John in the following table before we consider the pertinent details:

John	The Theme in a Christocentric World
1	The Enhumanization and the New World Order
2:1–11	Cleansing
2–4	Holy Space
5	The Sabbath
6–8	Mosaic Holy History
8	Relationship with Abraham
9	The Struggle between the Followers of Jesus and Those Who Follow Moses and Reject Jesus
10	Holy Land
11–12	Life in Light of the Death and Resurrection of Jesus

---

18. Richardson and Bowden, *Westminster Dictionary of Christian Theology*, 169.

The book of signs (chs. 1–12) starts with the enhumanization and ends with the death/resurrection of Christ. It consists of seven signs: transforming water into wine (2:1–11), healing the royal official's son in Capernaum (4:46–54), healing the paralytic at Bethesda (5:1–15), feeding the five thousand (6:1–14), Jesus walking on the water (6:16–24), healing the man blind from birth (9:1–7), and raising Lazarus (11:1–45). John informs us that these signs were written so that people may believe that Jesus is the Messiah, the Son of God, and that by believing they may have life in his name (20:31).

Similarly, the book of the hour (chs. 13–21) starts with servant leadership (ch. 13) which is associated with the enhumanization and ends with Jesus's death/resurrection (chs. 18–21). The hour refers to the crucifixion of Christ, his death, and resurrection. In the book of the hour, we encounter the following identities of the followers of the Christ:

Chapter	Main Identity Encountered
13	The People of Love
14, 16	The People of the Spirit
15–16	The Persecuted People
15	The People of the Vine
17	The People of Unity
18–19	The People of the Cross
20–21	The People of Resurrection

1

A New Beginning

After outlining the book of John in the introduction, it is time to unpack its details, beginning with an explanation of the new world order that dawned with the messianic age when Christ was born.[1] This new world order, rooted in the Old Testament, fulfills the dreams of the Old Testament prophets. It is the age they hoped for – the Davidic or messianic age in which the divine promises would be fulfilled, exile would end, and human beings would experience joy, freedom, and divine covenantal grace (Ezek 34:23; 37:24). It is the divine season when God's glory would be revealed and seen by all (Isa 40:5). It is the fullness of time in which the people walking in darkness would see a great light (Isa 9:2). It is the age in which the God of heaven would set up a kingdom that would never be destroyed (Dan 2:44).

From a Christian perspective, this is the messianic age that dawned when Christ came, the kingdom that Christ embodied and preached. John invites us to reflect on this issue from the perspective of the God who became human, from a christocentric point of view. His insistence on the centrality of Christ raises questions related to understanding the Old Testament and the role of biblical Israel. Such reflections are important, especially in light of theological discussions concerned with the relationship of the messianic age to the state of Israel or with seeing the state of Israel as the fulfillment of certain Old Testament prophecies. These discussions are crucial in Israel/Palestine.[2]

Our investigation of John's perception of the messianic age looks first at his introduction in chapter 1. Scholars agree that both Genesis in the Septuagint and the Gospel of John have similar beginnings.[3] Both books open with the

---

1. For further information about the hopes of the Old Testament for a messianic age, see Hoekema, *Bible and the Future*.

2. I have addressed this issue in Katanacho, *Land of Christ*.

3. Beasley-Murray, *John*, 10; Suggit, "Jesus the Gardner"; Spence-Jones, *Pulpit Commentary*; Borgen, "Logos"; Wright, *John for Everyone*.

phrase: "In the beginning." Genesis 1:1 says, "In the beginning God created the heavens and the earth," while John 1:1 says, "In the beginning was the Word." Genesis chapter 1 describes the role of God's spoken word in creating the world and everything in it and also discusses the themes of life and light. The same themes appear in the Gospel of John. However, life and light are related to the Word of God who became human.

Theology is thus associated with anthropology and cosmology. John is providing christological cosmology and is structuring the whole world around Christ, who is fully human and fully God.[4]

Some interpreters argue that the similarity between the two biblical books includes John's structuring of his discourse in seven days. In Genesis, God created the world in six days and rested on the seventh day. In the Gospel of John, the Jews of Jerusalem ask John the Baptist about his identity on the first day (1:19–28); then, we encounter the expression "on the next day" several times (1:29, 35–43). It is possible to suggest that each time the expression "on the next day" occurs it refers to another day. Thus, we have four days total. If the wedding at Cana is on the third day (2:1) from the fourth day, it is then on the seventh day (four plus three).[5] More similarities to the book of Genesis can be seen in the account of the wedding at Cana, as will be further explored later.

Regardless of our understanding of the days mentioned in John, we cannot ignore the emphasis on the new age or era that John is advancing. The Gospel declares that God became human; he entered our world through the womb of the Blessed Virgin. I prefer the use of the word "human" instead of the word "flesh," as the former highlights the reality that Jesus became fully human, not only that he received a human body.

Put differently, the invisible God became visible (1:18). The Holy One who could not be touched became one of us (1:14). The God of the whole universe became a citizen of an insignificant town, thus demonstrating his humility. He became human in the womb of a virgin living in Nazareth, a town that had less than 480 people.[6] Nazareth is the place where God became human and Bethlehem is the place where he was born.

Stated differently still, the second person of the Trinity became human. We touched him, we saw him, we heard him, and we saw his glory. Because of the incarnated God, we have seen the Father (14:9) and the Spirit (1:32–33). The Holy Spirit appeared and rested on Jesus. The Son of God became human and

---

4. Rushton, "Cosmology of John."

5. Carson, *Gospel According to John*, 168; Kim, "Relationship."

6. Strange, "Nazareth," 4:1050.

dwelt amongst us; the Spirit of God came down at his baptism, and the heavens opened up; the angels of God ascended and descended (1:51). This angelic scene expresses a new era, a divine moment that will last forever in Christ. We also read the words of Jesus, "Behold an Israelite without deceit" (1:47). The ascending and descending angels together with the expression "Israel" echo the story of Jacob in which we encounter ascending and descending angels as well as a man called Israel. It is helpful to explore the details of this story, and so we shall.

Jacob desired to steal the blessing that belonged to his brother. Therefore, he went to Isaac, their blind father, and impersonated Esau in order to receive his older brother's blessing. His father was indeed deceived. When Esau heard what had happened, he was full of rage and decided to kill his brother. Jacob ran away as far as possible to escape. When he got tired, he slept in a place that he later named Bethel, the house of God (Gen 28:10–22). At Bethel, he dreamed. In his dream he saw angels ascending and descending upon a ladder and the Lord standing at the top of the ladder. The dream was connected to the Abrahamic promise, which included the Abrahamic blessing, the land, and divine care. In that dream, Jacob heard God saying:

> I am the Lord, the God of Abraham your father and the God of Isaac; the land on which you lie I will give to you and to your descendants; and your descendants shall be like the dust of the earth, and you shall spread abroad to the west and to the east and to the north and to the south; and by you and your descendants shall all the families of the earth bless themselves. Behold, I am with you and will keep you wherever you go, and will bring you back to this land; for I will not leave you until I have done that of which I have spoken to you. (Gen 28:13–15)

When Jacob woke up, he called the place the "house of God" and the "gate of heaven."

This story is important if we are to understand the discourse between Jesus and Nathanael. The similarities between the two stories are compelling. In the account of Jacob and Esau, we see that Jacob is known to be deceitful. When Isaac explained to Esau what his younger brother had done, he said, "Your brother came deceitfully and took your blessing." Esau said, "Isn't he rightly named Jacob? This is the second time he has taken advantage of me: He took my birthright, and now he's taken my blessing!" (Gen 27:35–36). The birthright belongs to the firstborn son as he is the one who is responsible to lead the family, or the tribe, after the death of his father, and he receives two portions of the inheritance instead of one. Furthermore, the firstborn was the priest of the family who stood before God representing his family and who represented God before his family.[7] Jacob deceitfully took the birthright of Esau, and so his name is now connected to deceit. Nevertheless, by his grace, God lavished his blessings on Jacob.

Jesus brings this story to the first century and relates it to himself. Jesus, rather than Bethel, is now the house of God. Nathanael represents Israel (Jacob), but, unlike Jacob, he is without deceit. Instead of referring to the fulfillment of the Abrahamic promise through Jacob, Jesus is declared as king of Israel. Put differently, the king of Israel has come and shall establish the kingdom of God on earth. In some manuscripts the first chapter of John ends with the words "from now" or "hereafter," pointing to the dawn of a new age.[8]

A new era is dawning, one in which the heavens are connected to the earth through the God who became human. The secrets of the Father are now revealed by the Son. Jesus explains the Father in a perfect way. John states, "No one has ever seen God; the only Son, who is in the bosom of the Father, he has made him known" (1:18). The expression "made him known" means to have elaborated and explained accurately. John unpacks the way Jesus reveals the Father via seven signs in the book of signs (chs. 1–12).[9]

It is important to distinguish between a miracle, a wonder, acts of power, and a sign: (1) A miracle refers to the supernatural. It cannot be explained by scientific or natural laws. (2) A wonder creates a response in which we marvel. (3) Acts of power require investments of power beyond human capacity. (4) Finally, a sign is a thing that points to something else. The signs in John refer to the dawning of the Davidic age, the identity of Jesus, and belief in him (20:31). In Christ, the promises of the Old Testament are fulfilled. He is the king of Israel. To unpack this new beginning that starts in Jesus, we shall now discuss the first sign, the wedding at Cana.

---

7. Davis, "Israel's Inheritance," 79.

8. For further details, see the footnote of verse 51 in Nestle-Aland, *Novum Testamentum Graece*, 296.

9. Dodd, *Interpretation of the Fourth Gospel*, x.

Discussion Questions

1. The introduction spoke of the "lenses" we bring to the reading of Scripture. As we begin to explore the Gospel of John, what are the lenses – the mindsets and assumptions – that you bring to the text? What factors – cultural, political, denominational, or other – shape, and enrich, your own perspective?

2. Why is it important to encounter Scripture not just from your own perspective but from the perspective of others?

3. Take a moment to compare the beginning of Genesis with the beginning of the Gospel of John. What parallels do you notice in words, ideas, and themes? What do you think is John's purpose in drawing so many parallels? What is he hoping the reader will think, question, or notice?

4. Reflect over John 1. How does this first chapter set the stage for the coming of the Davidic – the messianic – age?

5. Do you agree with the distinctions drawn between miracles, wonders, acts of power, and signs? If so, what is the significance of labeling the acts of Christ, in the Gospel of John, not miracles or wonders, but signs? If they are signs, what does that require of us, the reader? How should we respond?

2

The Sign of the Wedding of Cana

The wedding at Cana, the first sign in the Gospel of John, addresses the new beginning. It is indeed interesting to reflect on this wedding in light of the similarities between the Gospel of John and the book of Genesis. The latter book describes the relationship of the first couple, Adam and Eve, while John presents a wedding in Cana, the first in a series of signs. John's rendering is similar to Genesis in that he presents God's work with humanity as beginning with a couple. John's account of a wedding paves the way for the introduction of the dawn of a new age, a messianic age. First-century Jewish weddings were replete with symbolism that pointed to God's relationship with Israel. Thus, it is significant that the first sign in the Gospel of John was a wedding, and, more specifically, that the wedding occurred on the third day (2:1).

There are several ways to understand the phrase "on the third day." First, we can focus on its linguistic and historical meanings. In Jewish culture, the third day is Tuesday. Jews call Sunday *Yom Rishon*, which means the first day; Monday is *Yom Shini*, the second day; Tuesday is *Yom Shlishi*, the third day, etc. Usually, Jews in the first century married in the middle of the week because they wanted to avoid violating the laws of the Sabbath. Law keepers insisted on having enough time to prepare for weddings without profaning the Sabbath, while it was also considered wise to avoid the Sabbath in case the court needed to be convened (if, for instance, the groom claimed his bride was not a virgin).[1]

In concord with getting married in the middle of the week, some Jews believed that the third day is the best day to marry, as the use of the word "good" in Genesis occurs only once on the first, fourth, and fifth days, does not occur at all on the second day, but is used twice on the third and sixth days (Gen 1:1–31).

---

1. See b. Ketub. 2a ("Ketubot 2a:1–11," *The William Davidson Talmud*, Sefaria, https://www.sefaria.org/Ketubot.2a.1-11?lang=bi).

Second, we can reflect on the phrase "on the third day" from a literary point of view. If we count this as the third day after the four days mentioned in chapter 1, perhaps John is presenting seven days. On the first day, John the Baptist declares that he is not the Messiah but a voice that precedes the coming of the Lord (1:19). On the second day (1:29), we witness the baptism of Jesus and the appearance of the Spirit of God. On that day, John the Baptist declares that Jesus is the Lamb of God who takes away the sin of the world and baptizes with the Holy Spirit. On the third day (1:35), Andrew and Simon find the Messiah. On the fourth day (1:43), Philip and Nathanael follow the Son of God (also referred to as the king of Israel and the Son of Man). Looking at the chronology of the days in chapter 1, it is possible to suggest that the expression "on the third day" at the beginning of the second chapter of John is used in relation to the days mentioned in chapter 1. From this perspective, the third day at the beginning of chapter 2 is connected to the fourth day in chapter 1 – that is, it is the seventh day. Chapter 1 ends with a scene in which Jesus engages Nathanael from Cana (cf. 21:2), promising him that he would see greater divine acts (1:50). Chapter 2 is a fulfillment of that promise and takes place in the town of Cana, Nathanael's hometown. If the sign happened on the third day from the fourth day, we add four and three which equals seven. This suggestion might have theological significance in light of the similarities between the beginnings of the Gospel of John and the book of Genesis.

Third, John wrote his gospel decades after the resurrection of Christ. During the time he wrote, the connection between the expression "on the third day" and the resurrection of Christ was widespread. Let us consider biblical examples that preceded the Gospel of John. The apostle Peter went to the house of Cornelius and preached that Christ was raised from the dead on the third day (Acts 10:40). The apostle Paul stated that the buried Christ was raised on the third day according to the Scriptures (1 Cor 15:3). High priests, Pharisees, and Pilate knew about the third day (Matt 27:62–64).

Put differently, it is possible that the expression "on the third day" in the account of the wedding at Cana provokes thoughts about the resurrection of Christ. This possibility increases in light of the interpretation of the first sign presented below. It also increases because Christians connected the redemption of Christ with wedding symbolism. They perceived Christ as the groom (3:29) and the church as his bride. Even if one dismisses the symbolic connection between the third day and the resurrection of Christ, we argue that it would be difficult to avoid the connection between the wedding at Cana and the redemption of Christ.

God's interaction with human beings in the Old Testament began when he established marriage and officiated the wedding of Adam and Eve. Their presiding pastor was God himself. The children of Israel perceived this first wedding as a divine act and consequently developed important religious interpretations and social customs surrounding the marriage ceremony.[2] Although the uncritical endorsement of first-century customs is not necessary, understanding those customs does help us better understand the wedding at Cana.

A wedding was a covenant between two families or countries. Usually, the father of the groom would discuss the conditions of the marriage with the father of the bride. The groom's family would present gifts to the bride and her family as part of the engagement (see Gen 24:53). This was followed by a written agreement, but the couple was not yet allowed to consummate the marriage with sexual intercourse as husband and wife. The bride and groom continued to live apart, each in their parents' home, until the consummation day, which occurred during a week-long celebration (see Judg 14:10–12; Gen 29:21–27). The events of the celebration were as follows: the groom and his friends went to the bride's house; then, in a special bedchamber, he removed the veil covering her face and knew her as his wife. They would then spend the night in the bedchamber while the couple's friends and the bride's parents celebrated outside. In the morning, after the consummation of marriage, the best friends would check the bedchamber and linens in order to testify to the virginity of the bride. They would then present the bloodstained cloth to the parents of the bride (see Deut 22:17).[3] Later, the couple left the bride's house and went to the wedding feast at the groom's house.

It is important to imagine the wedding as accurately as possible. The bride, for example, did not wear a white dress in the first century. In AD 1406, Philippa of England was one of the first women in recorded history to wear a white wedding dress. In AD 1559, Mary Queen of Scotland was married in a white wedding gown, and later, in 1840, the white gown was popularized by Queen Victoria.[4] In Jewish first-century culture, brides wore blue or purple dresses as the groom and bride were treated as a king and queen. As his friends accompanied the groom to the bride's house, they played flutes, tambourines, and drums, and they sang, danced, pronounced blessings, and recited poetry

---

2. Perkin, "Marriage."

3. Sadly, these oppressive customs continue to this very day in certain villages in Egypt!

4. Danesi, *Semiotics of Love*, 152.

on their way (see Ruth 4:11–12; Song of Songs 3:6–11; Ps 45).[5] Then the couple returned to the groom's house to continue the celebrations.[6]

A wedding was attended by three kinds of invitees: family members and friends, the poor, and the rich or dignitaries. First, family members and friends were expected to bring gifts, the value of which would be reciprocated when they hosted a wedding. For example, if a family member or friend gave a gift valued at one hundred dollars, they would expect a gift of at least one hundred dollars in return when they invited this family to a wedding in their family. To bring a gift of less worth was considered shameful. In other words, gifts given by family members and friends were considered to be a kind of social debt that would be returned on another happy occasion.

Second, the poor also attended weddings; they ate and drank freely but were not expected to give any gifts. Third, rich people or dignitaries were also invited and were expected to give large gifts according to their social status, usually wine. They gave unconditional gifts, expecting nothing in return. When Jesus appeared at the wedding, people wondered what his social status was and what kind of gift he would give. Some thought that he was a relative as his mother was in the kitchen helping with wedding arrangements, while others thought that he was poor and could not offer a gift.

In any case, the wine ran out, which was a serious problem in a first-century Jewish wedding. The reputation of the family was at stake. Reputation was more important than wealth. Furthermore, due to the corruption of certain people who used weddings to receive gifts and gain income without providing food, first-century rabbis responded with strict laws. If a person presented a gift at a wedding where there was insufficient food or drink, then that person could take the groom to court. If the latter was found guilty, he would be imprisoned.[7] Thus, the couple encountered a serious problem that could have destroyed their marriage. Their wedding could have been transformed from joy to sadness, and the status of the groom could have been overturned from a king to a condemned prisoner. However, as Jesus intervened and changed water into wine, the problem became an opportunity to reveal the glory of Christ, and, in so doing, he gave the couple a great, free and unconditional gift. He asked the servants to fill the water jars to the brim to demonstrate that there were no tricks involved – no one could add any liquid to the filled jars. When

---

5. Towner, "Wedding," 1125–1126.

6. These details can help us better understand the parable of the ten virgins and the bridegroom who was late (Matt 25:1–13).

7. Hayden, *When the Good News*, 44; Crutcher, *That He Might Be Revealed*, 89; Derrett, *Law*, 228–246.

Jesus transformed the water into wine, he gave them more than five hundred bottles of good wine, demonstrating that his gift was similar to those of great dignitaries. It was a free, unconditional gift that the couple would remember for the rest of their lives.

Christ solved a serious problem at the wedding, but he created another serious one. There was no longer water at the wedding. The water jars were used for purification, and the jars were large enough to contain the quantity of water needed for all the purification required. The people had to wash their hands, the utensils, and more. Some washed their hands before the meal, during the meal, and after it. Purification reflected their commitment to obey the law of Moses. How would the guests be purified? They had six water jars, one for every day.[8] They could rest from these rituals only on the Sabbath.

In order to better understand John's intentions, it might be helpful to look at the motif of water in the Gospel of John.[9] We encounter the water of baptism in chapter 1; in chapter 2, water is transformed into wine; in chapter 3, Jesus challenges Nicodemus to be born again from water and the Spirit; in chapter 4, Christ offers the Samaritan woman water that wells up into eternal life; in chapter 5, we encounter a sign next to a pool; in chapter 6, Jesus walks on the water; in chapter 7, Jesus relates the living water to the Holy Spirit; in chapter 9, Jesus asks the man born blind to go and wash in the pool of Siloam; in John 11 (v. 55), the text reminds us of the importance of cleansing; in chapter 13, Jesus washes the feet of the disciples; and in John 19, when Jesus is pierced, water and blood come out of his side. It seems that John is indeed interested in the water motif.

In the second chapter of John, the reference to water is part of a larger water motif that concerns the requirement of water for purification. The Bible informs us that there were six water jars for purification (2:6). Also, we know that the servants filled the jars to the brim and all the water was transformed into wine. Put differently, Jesus solved the problem of the absence of wine but created a new problem, the absence of cleansing water. This idea becomes more significant in light of its context, for the wedding at Cana in the first part of John 2 is juxtaposed with the cleansing of the temple – and Jesus's statements about its destruction and replacement – in the second part of John 2.[10]

---

8. El Meskeen (المسكين), الإنجيل بحسب القديس يوحنا [The Gospel According to St John], 174.

9. Ng, *Water Symbolism in John*.

10. This is unlike the Synoptic Gospels, which place the cleansing of the temple at the end of the ministry of Jesus. We shall address the topic of replacing the temple in chapter 3.

It is thus legitimate to ask: If there is no cleansing water, how will people be purified? The Gospel of John presents several interconnected themes. When we trace some of these motifs through words, imagery, and other literary tools, then we have a better understanding. One of the important words in the story of the wedding at Cana is the word "hour." Jesus told his mother that his hour had not yet come (2:4), but, at the same time, he performed a sign that resolved the problem of the lack of wine. Why did he speak in such a way? Perhaps Jesus is indicating that the foundation of the coming messianic or Davidic age is not to be miracles but the "hour." The "hour" is a clear motif in the Gospel of John, connected to the glory of Christ, his suffering, death, resurrection, and the redemption of humanity, as mentioned explicitly in 7:30, 12:23–27, 13:1, and 17:1.

Reference	The text from the NIV translation
John 7:30	At this they tried to seize him, but no one laid a hand on him, because his hour had not yet come.
John 12:23	Jesus replied, "The hour has come for the Son of Man to be glorified."
John 12:27	"Now my soul is troubled, and what shall I say? 'Father, save me from this hour'? No, it was for this very reason I came to this hour."
John 13:1	It was just before the Passover Festival. Jesus knew that the hour had come for him to leave this world and go to the Father. Having loved his own who were in the world, he loved them to the end.
John 17:1	After Jesus said this, he looked toward heaven and prayed: "Father, the hour has come. Glorify your Son, that your Son may glorify you."

When we read the above texts together, we recognize that the motif of the hour in the Gospel of John is related to the cross as well as the glorification of Jesus through the cross. The "hour" becomes an indispensable foundation for the messianic or Davidic age and is the prerequisite for the new world order. The water of purification in first-century Pharisaic Judaism would not be transformed into the messianic wine without the dawn of the hour. The messianic activity that is centered on the hour becomes the starting point for rereading the major elements of John's perception of Pharisaic Judaism. Assuming this perspective in reading the first sign, we recognize that the glory of Christ would not be revealed without the cross as well as the resurrection. Therefore, it is important to stress that John presents signs, not miracles, and that these signs pave the way for a better understanding of the messianic age and the kingdom of God.

Signs alone are not enough to lead people to a saving faith or even to a discovery of the crucified God. Jesus performed many signs in Jerusalem on the Passover. Many believed in his name, but Jesus did not entrust himself to them (2:23–25). Nicodemus was interested in Christ because of the signs, but he could not discover the identity of the savior of the world (see ch. 3). In addition, the crowds saw many signs but were not satisfied and did not discover God (6:25–31). When the high priests and other first-century Jewish leaders met in a council to discuss the resurrection of Lazarus, they admitted that Jesus had performed many signs. Although they accepted that the signs were genuine, they decided to kill Jesus (11:47–53). Signs are not enough! The way to discover the glory of God is through the death and resurrection of the Messiah. Only this way will change history and offer to God the glory he deserves.

Put differently, Christ honored the request of his mother at the wedding at Cana, but he insisted on the way of the cross: "'Woman, why do you involve me?' Jesus replied. 'My hour has not yet come'" (John 2:4).[11] Jesus did not rebuke his mother but rather respected her desire. At the same time, he expressed his unbending commitment to revealing his glory through his crucifixion and resurrection He rescued the couple in Cana from social humiliation without abandoning his commitment to the cross. The cross is the way to reveal the glory of God and a new world order in which changes start by the transformation of hearts, not mere behavioral changes. Thus, the "hour," or the death and resurrection of the Christ, becomes the lens through which we see the enhumanization of the second person of the Trinity. It also becomes the mindset or worldview that interprets the identity and works of the Christ. We can no longer understand the humanity of Christ only from the perspective of his conception and birth. We must also consider his humanity in relation to the cross and resurrection.

In other words, Jesus was not only a Jewish baby; he was also the savior of the world. He was not only shaped by first-century Judaism; he also redefined many central components of Jewishness. He was the groom of the messianic age in whom the longings of Old Testament prophets were fulfilled. John the Baptist said, "I am not the Messiah but am sent ahead of him. The bride belongs to the bridegroom. The friend who attends the bridegroom waits and listens

---

11. The expression "woman" is not derogatory. John uses it in 2:4; 4:21; 8:10; 19:26; 20:13, 25. John usually uses it to respectfully call upon a woman in trouble. For further information about the expression "woman" in John 2:4, see Bulembat, "Head-Waiter and Bridegroom."

for him, and is full of joy when he hears the bridegroom's voice. That joy is mine, and it is now complete" (3:28–29). Christ, the groom, redeems his bride through the cross; thus, the motif of the hour is related to Christ, the groom. The connection between the sign of the wedding at Cana and the cleansing of the temple becomes clearer as we reflect on Christ, the groom, who redeemed us through the cross, where his body was broken and his blood was spilled. The signs in the Gospel of John must be connected to this central reality.

Only his death and resurrection provide a lasting meaning to his signs. John explicitly connects the death of Christ to signs. He quotes the Jews saying, "What sign can you show us to prove your authority to do all this?" (2:18). The response was the death and resurrection of Christ (2:19–22). In light of this discussion, the dawn of the messianic age, and the new world order, it is fitting to develop our understanding of the temple and holy space in the Gospel of John. How did the coming of Christ affect the concept of holy space?

Discussion Questions

1. What are the wedding traditions of your own culture, and how are they similar to, or different than, those of first-century Palestine?

2. If this narrative were to be translated into your own cultural context, what crisis might Christ have encountered, and how might he have used that crisis to bless the marriage and point towards his own identity?

3. If the third day is meant to be taken as an allusion to the resurrection of Christ, what significance might that allusion contain?

4. Why do you think it might matter that God began his work, in Genesis, with Adam and Eve, and Christ begins his work, in the Gospel of John, with a wedding?

5. Read the account in John of the cleansing of the temple (John 2:13–22). Why do you think John chooses to juxtapose these two scenes? What bearing does the water turned to wine have on the story of the temple cleansing?

6. How does the wedding at Cana act as a sign? How does it point to the nature of Christ, his work, and his kingdom? What might it teach us about Christ and who we are called to be as his church?

3

Holy Space

Many Jews and Zionist Christians talk about rebuilding the temple, and they connect the plan of God with the building of a third temple for the Jews.[1] Thus, the promises and dreams of the Old Testament would be fulfilled in a literal way. The promises and warnings concerning the Jews and the nations would come to fulfillment, including a great tribulation followed by a millennium of peace. From this perspective, the prophecies concerning geography are literal.

But what does John think about holy space? How can we understand holy space in light of the new world order? We have already spoken about the inclusive Christ whom John introduces by rereading the basic components of Pharisaic Judaism in relation to the centrality of Jesus Christ. But what is the specific relationship of the temple – or holy space – to this inclusive Christ? What is the relationship of the temple of stones to the temple of flesh – that is, to Jesus Christ in whom the good news is embodied?

No doubt the temple was important and central during the second temple period. Since the return of the Jews from exile in the sixth century BC until the destruction of the temple in AD 70, the temple was – according to most Jews – the place where God dwelt. It was the center of religious life and the place where forgiveness was found. It embodied the history of the relationship between God and his people. It reflected God's faithfulness to his people throughout time. It also embodied the future dream in which all nations would come to the house of the Lord and wars would be no more.

The temple, indispensable for defining the identity of most faithful Jews in first-century Judaism, was their religious and political flag. If the people lost the temple, they would lose their identity, history, blessings, stability, and

---

1. See Inbari, *Jewish Fundamentalism*.

religious life, and would live in exile and alienation. Losing the temple was like crucifixion without resurrection. It was the death of God and the victory of evil.

Therefore, we must listen well when the text speaks about destroying the temple. Imagine someone speaking to Muslims about destroying the Kaaba in Saudi Arabia or to Catholics about demolishing the Church of the Holy Sepulcher or the Vatican! Christ said to the Jews of Jerusalem, "Destroy this temple, and I will raise it again in three days" (2:19). These unforgettable statements continued to bother first-century Jews and became vivid when their leaders judged Jesus. Matthew informs us that, during the tribunal of Jesus, some testified that he had said, "I am able to destroy the temple of God and rebuild it in three days" (Matt 26:61). The Gospel of Mark says, "Some stood up and gave this false testimony against him: We heard him say, I will destroy this temple made with human hands and in three days will build another, not made with hands" (Mark 14:57–58). It is clear that the words of Jesus about the temple made a big impact on many Jews and were presented as justification for condemning him to death.

In order to further clarify the discussion in John, we need to unpack the temple's historical background. When Jerusalem fell into the hands of Antiochus in the second century BC, that tyrant and the Seleucids imposed Hellenization on the Jews. Antiochus Epiphanes, the eighth ruler of the Seleucid Empire, ordered the Jews to worship his gods in Jerusalem. In 167 BC, he erected a statue to Zeus, then sacrificed a pig on the altar in the temple, prohibited temple worship, and forbade circumcision (see 1 Mac 1:29–64; 2 Mac 6:1–9). These events led to the Maccabean revolt. The Maccabeans liberated and purified the temple in 164 BC and built a new altar (1 Mac 4:36–61; 2 Mac 10:1–8). They celebrated for eight days (1 Mac 4:56; 2 Mac 10:6), an explosion of joy that in time became an annual celebration (1 Mac 4:59; 2 Mac 10:8).

The Gospel of John calls this annual celebration the Feast of Dedication (10:22), and Jews today celebrate this feast as Hanukkah. When the temple was liberated from the Gentiles, the Jews celebrated Hanukkah or the rededication of the temple with palm branches (1 Mac 10:7). This is an important background detail that relates to the entry of Jesus into Jerusalem in the Synoptic Gospels. These gospels associated his entry with palm branches and with the cleansing of the temple (see Matt 21:1–17; Mark 11:1–19; Luke 21:28–48). It is no surprise that his entry into Jerusalem was followed by cleansing the temple and expelling those who turned the house of prayer into a den of thieves. Surprisingly, he does not expel Gentiles. Rather, he drives out Jewish offenders, insisting that the house of God is a place for holiness and divine presence, not for trading or defilement.[2]

In any case, it is interesting that the Gospel of John places the cleansing of the temple immediately after the wedding at Cana in order to highlight the new world order which dawns with the coming of the Messiah. Would the age of the temple come to an end? John informs us that Jesus is the temple (2:21). This statement is contextually significant, especially in light of the wedding at Cana and the historical correlation between cleansing the temple and the entry into Jerusalem.

Unlike the Synoptic Gospels, John places the temple discourse between the wedding at Cana and the story of Nicodemus in order to highlight the new age to come in which Jesus replaces the temple. This Johannine declaration is important in Israel/Palestine today since both Muslims and Jews emphasize the importance of holy space and fight over the Temple Mount area. Some Christians also advocate the building of a third temple, even if it entails the bloodshed of many Palestinians and Israelis.

In light of the aforementioned brief historical background, the literary context can be understood more accurately. John presents holy space within a larger argument that relates to a new world order. The literary context begins with the first sign (2:11) and ends with the second sign (4:54). The wedding at Cana is mentioned at the beginning and at the end of this literary unit. Interestingly, John 4:46 states, "Once more he visited Cana in Galilee, where he had turned the water into wine." The text also connects us to what Jesus had done in Jerusalem saying, "When he arrived in Galilee, the Galileans welcomed him. They had seen all that he had done in Jerusalem at the Passover Festival, for they also had been there" (4:45).

We find in this literary unit a comparison between Jews and Gentiles. The Jews wanted to see a sign in order to believe (2:18). Their faith was not trustworthy (2:23–25). By the end of the pertinent literary unit, Christ rebukes his hearers saying, "Unless you people see signs and wonders . . . you will never believe" (4:48). In the same context, we encounter the faith of the servant of the king who believed in Jesus along with his household. This gentile leader responded to Jesus better than most first-century Jerusalemite Jews. He believed in Jesus and understood his power to grant life. The same literary unit elaborates this kind of comparison by highlighting the differences between Nicodemus and the Samaritan woman.

---

2. Wright, *Jesus and the Victory*, 413–428.

Nicodemus	Samaritan
Man	Woman
Jew	Samaritan
A leader of the Jews	A woman without a husband
He saw signs	She did not see signs
He came at night	She came in the middle of the day
He did not accept the testimony of Christ	She testified about Christ
Christ is a rabbi or a teacher	Christ is the savior of the world

Several scholars point out the lower social status of the Samaritan woman. She was a second-class citizen in a patriarchal first-century culture. The fourth chapter, which unpacks the story of a despised Samaritan woman, is read in the context of the third chapter, which mentions a prominent Jewish leader.[3] This leader comes to Jesus at night (an hour that has negative connotations in the Gospel of John), while the woman comes to Jesus at noon. The Jewish leader accepts Jesus partially, but the woman confesses that Jesus is not only the Messiah but also the savior of the world. In brief, John encourages us to compare these two figures.

Such a comparison would not be complete, however, if we ignored holy space, a central idea in John 4:20–25. Moreover, in the third chapter, Jesus informs Nicodemus that the presence of the Spirit of God is not limited to one place. He says, "The wind blows wherever it pleases. You hear its sound, but you cannot tell where it comes from or where it is going. So it is with everyone born of the Spirit" (3:8). The word "wind" in Greek can also be translated as "Spirit" or "spirit." Therefore, it is possible to argue that the Spirit blows wherever it pleases. The work of God cannot be limited to one place. It can be in everyplace, and those who are born of the Spirit can also be in any place.

This claim about holy space and its connection to the Spirit is elaborated in the discussion of Jesus and the Samaritan woman. The Spirit of God is not found only in one place. Furthermore, the temple area is no longer necessary in order to worship the Father properly. First-century Judaism lost its monopoly over the place of worship, for the followers of God should focus on the nature of worship rather than on the place of worship. Worshipers can fully please God even if they don't worship on the Temple Mount.

Clearly, the nature of God is the determining factor in shaping the worship of God. This is the divine nature that is revealed in Jesus Christ and is not

---

3. Pazdan, "Nicodemus and the Samaritan."

limited to a specific place of worship. In fact, John has already alluded to this reality when he declared that the Word became human and made his dwelling among us (1:14). The expression "made his dwelling" refers to a specific location for a tent. Jesus has become the tent of meeting with God. He is the temple and the house of God.[4] Those who have known him have known God. Those who have seen him have seen God (14:5–10). Furthermore, John reminds us in 1:51 of the ladder of Jacob and the house of God. Jesus is introduced as the true house of God where the angels are ascending and descending.

This approach challenges the teachings of Judaism and Islam, and it also challenges the claim that the Temple Mount (with or without a temple) is the actual place where God will reside in the future. In short, the humanity of Jesus is the place where God and human beings meet, where we see the face of God. It is the space in which human beings reconcile with God. Humanity and divinity are fully reconciled in Jesus Christ who is fully God and fully human. He is the only way for such reconciliation. Put differently, the house of God is a human being and is accessible to all human beings. All are equally called to believe in him. There is no place for pride or ethnic superiority or exclusion. There is no longer a need to argue about the holiest places on earth. Is Mecca holier than Rome or Jerusalem holier than Constantinople? In the new world order, the nature of God determines the nature of his worship. Holy space is now associated with Jesus Christ and therefore influences the holy calendar. The relationship between holy space and holy seasons is intimate. The most sacred seasons were associated with the temple in Jerusalem. Viewing holy space in relation to Christ raises new questions about holy time.

---

4. See Hoskins, *Jesus as the Fulfillment.*

Discussion Questions

1. What is the center of religious life for your own community? Does Jesus's teaching about the temple challenge your community's sense of what is central? Should it? If so, how so?

2. Jesus contrasts his interactions with Nicodemus, a Pharisee and religious leader, and the Samaritan woman, an outcast. What would be equivalent roles in your own community? By depicting the Samaritan woman as someone who accepts Christ fully, while Nicodemus holds back, how is Christ challenging our perceptions of – and engagement with – others?

3. What is your perspective on holy space? If you had been present when Jesus declared that he would destroy the temple, what do you think your response might have been?

4. If Jesus *is* holy space – if he has become the temple, the tent of meeting, etc. – what are the implications for us as his followers? How should we relate to physical forms of holy space? What should we believe about them?

4

Holy Time

The right relationship with God in the Old Testament was intimately connected with a specific geographical location as well as with a holy calendar.[1] This calendar shaped the worship that was offered to the Lord of the universe. The children of Israel appeared before the Lord three times a year to renew their covenant (Exod 34:23). Their worship was diverse. Some days were joyful while others were sad.[2]

One of the things that has not changed is the centrality of the Sabbath, which is still considered a major marker on every Jewish calendar. A day of worship, it is the first holy day mentioned in the Torah. The Bible states, "By the seventh day God had finished the work he had been doing; so on the seventh day he rested from all his work. Then God blessed the seventh day and made it holy, because on it he rested from all the work of creating that he had done" (Gen 2:2–3). The Sabbath was also the sign of Israel's covenant with God. Despising the Sabbath meant despising God's covenant and undervaluing the calling of Israel to be distinct. Indeed, God sanctified Israel and made her into a kingdom of priests, a holy nation, and a treasured possession (Exod 19:5–6). The Sabbath was a reminder of all these realities. The Bible states:

> Say to the Israelites, You must observe my Sabbaths. This will be a sign between me and you for the generations to come, so you may know that I am the Lord, who makes you holy. Observe the Sabbath, because it is holy to you. Anyone who desecrates it is to be put to death; those who do any work on that day must be cut off from their people. For six days work is to be done, but the seventh day is a day of Sabbath rest, holy to the Lord. Whoever does any work on the Sabbath day is to be put to death. The Israelites are

1. Wright, "Feasts, Festivals, and Fasts."
2. Harrison, "Feasts and Festivals."

> to observe the Sabbath, celebrating it for the generations to come
> as a lasting covenant. (Exod 31:13–16)

It is important to remember that this concept of holy time was associated with a system of worship rooted in a particular holy space. But Christ, in the Gospel of John, is now arguing that God is not only omnipresent but he can also be worshiped everywhere. With the change in perception of holy space comes a new way of looking at holy time. Thus, we can ask what John thinks about the Sabbath and how he reads the Sabbath in light of this new perspective.

As we have already seen, John deconstructs the concept of holy space in Pharisaic Judaism and reconstructs it in a way that highlights the centrality of Christ. Now, he continues the discussion by addressing holy time. As we have already pointed out, Jews have always highlighted a particular calendar in which the Sabbath is prominent and even central. Adele Reinhartz reminds us that the Sabbath is a foretaste of the coming age.[3] It is the day of rest and worship. It is the day in which we reorient ourselves around the centrality of God and commit ourselves to live accordingly. We commit ourselves to live in a way that pleases the Lord of the whole universe. The Sabbath is the space in which we reprioritize our lives in a way that is compatible with God's purposes. It is the time for empowering ourselves to resist all forms of slavery to idols.[4]

John mentions two signs that were enacted on a Sabbath: the healing of the crippled man at Bethesda (ch. 5) and the healing of the man born blind (ch. 9). Jesus healed a paralyzed person on the Sabbath and then asked the healed person to carry his mattress, also on the Sabbath. This provoked the anger of first-century Jerusalemite Jews since they were not allowed to carry such things on a Sabbath. The prophet Jeremiah says, "This is what the Lord says: Be careful not to carry a load on the Sabbath day or bring it through the gates of Jerusalem. Do not bring a load out of your houses or do any work on the Sabbath, but keep the Sabbath day holy, as I commanded your ancestors" (Jer 17:21–22). Nehemiah adds:

> In those days I saw people in Judah treading winepresses on the
> Sabbath and bringing in grain and loading it on donkeys, together
> with wine, grapes, figs and all other kinds of loads. And they
> were bringing all this into Jerusalem on the Sabbath. Therefore I
> warned them against selling food on that day. People from Tyre
> who lived in Jerusalem were bringing in fish and all kinds of

---

3. Reinhartz, *Befriending the Beloved Disciple*, 117.
4. For further details, see Brueggemann, *Sabbath as Resistance*.

merchandise and selling them in Jerusalem on the Sabbath to the people of Judah. I rebuked the nobles of Judah and said to them, "What is this wicked thing you are doing – desecrating the Sabbath day? Didn't your ancestors do the same things, so that our God brought all this calamity on us and on this city? Now you are stirring up more wrath against Israel by desecrating the Sabbath." (Neh 13:15–18)

Nehemiah associates the wrath of God against Israel with breaking the Sabbath. Thus, he ordered the people to close the gates of Jerusalem on the Sabbath in order to prevent all kinds of violations of the Sabbath. The Mishnah adds more details about breaking the Sabbath. It mentions thirty-nine forbidden tasks, saying:

> The principal acts of labor (prohibited on the Sabbath) are forty less one – viz.: Sowing, ploughing, reaping, binding into sheaves, threshing, winnowing, fruit-cleaning, grinding, sifting, kneading, baking, wool-shearing, bleaching, combing, dyeing, spinning, warping, making two spindle-trees, weaving two threads, separating two threads (in the warp), tying a knot, untying a knot, sewing on with two stitches, tearing in order to sew together with two stitches, hunting deer, slaughtering the same, skinning them, salting them, preparing the hide, scraping the hair off, cutting it, writing two (single) letters (characters), erasing in order to write two letters, building, demolishing (in order to rebuild), kindling, extinguishing (fire), hammering, transferring from one place into another. These are the principal acts of labor – forty less one.[5]

Although the Mishnah was written hundreds of years after the New Testament, it is fair to claim that many of the traditions written in the Mishnah were practiced before it was written and occupied a dominant space in oral rabbinic teachings. In short, carrying a mattress on a Sabbath was indeed problematic, especially in Jerusalem, the center of religious activities. The Jews said to the one who was carrying the mattress, "It is the Sabbath; the law forbids you to carry your mat" (5:10). And when they learned that the one who healed him was the one who asked him to carry his mat, they were furious. They wanted to kill Jesus because they believed that he had desecrated the Sabbath, despising the covenant with God, and must be punished by death (5:16).

---

5. Rodkinson, ed. *Babylonian Talmud*, 135–136.

The Jews did not want life to cease on the Sabbath, but they insisted that there should be no work. Thus, they posed several questions: What is work? What is lawful or unlawful on a Sabbath? Is carrying something for non-profit purposes lawful? Does God work on the Sabbath? If God works on the Sabbath, then he breaks the law, but if he doesn't, then who takes care of the world on the Sabbath? Several Jewish leaders argued that God works on the Sabbath without breaking the law, but Jesus's claim goes further. He demands to be viewed as God in relation to the Sabbath. He states, "My Father is always at his work to this very day, and I too am working" (5:17). The teachers of the law justified God working on the Sabbath, and now Jesus expects them to accept his work on the Sabbath as well.

It seems, then, that Jesus is claiming equality with the Father. John confirms this as he writes, "For this reason they tried all the more to kill him; not only was he breaking the Sabbath, but he was even calling God his own Father, making himself equal with God" (5:18). The Jews challenged him, but he did not back down. Instead, he affirmed the connection between his work and the Father's work on the Sabbath, as well as his equality with God.

He argued his position with a series of four reasons, as follows. It is of interest to note that the Greek text of these verses is structured around four statements, all of which use the Greek expression *gar*, which can be translated as "for" or "because." Jesus declares that he is equal to God, saying:

> Very truly I tell you, the Son can do nothing by himself; he can do only what he sees his Father doing, because whatever the Father does the Son also does. For the Father loves the Son and shows him all he does. Yes, and he will show him even greater works than these, so that you will be amazed. For just as the Father raises the dead and gives them life, even so the Son gives life to whom he is pleased to give it. Moreover, the Father judges no one, but has entrusted all judgment to the Son, that all may honor the Son just as they honor the Father. Whoever does not honor the Son does not honor the Father, who sent him. (5:19–23)

Christ insisted that his work and the work of the Father are one. He explains, "Whatever the Father does the Son also does." The Son is claiming that he can do what the Father does in terms of quality and mechanism. The Father can bring back to life whoever he wants, and so can the Son. If the Father brings someone back to life by one word, so does the Son. The first-century Jews believed that only God could bring the rain (Deut 28:12), open barren wombs

(Gen 30:22), and raise the dead (Ezek 37:13).[6] Jesus not only claims that he can raise the dead, he also asks his hearers to honor him as they honor God the Father, a claim made in the context of accusations against the notion that he was equal to God. Thus, it is evident in John that the Sabbath is connected to the work of the Father and the Son. It is also connected to the resurrection of the dead and judgment. As Christ says, "Whoever hears my word and believes him who sent me has eternal life and will not be judged but has crossed over from death to life" (5:24). This is the Sabbath, the true rest that Christ offers.

Christ argues that the purpose of the Sabbath is fulfilled through him, for in him people experience rest and life. Through him people receive healing, salvation, redemption, and rest. This is the Sabbath. It is the messianic age in which the promises are fulfilled. The Sabbath is associated with God's pleasure and satisfaction over his creation and his rest in an ideal world, as in the world of Genesis 1. But in a fallen world, the Sabbath is the dream of a coming age, and the eschatological hope for rest when our humanity is fully restored and we rest from our work (Heb 4:5–11).

God is not pleased with us without Christ; the eschatological Sabbath cannot exist without Jesus Christ. He is our Sabbath and the only perfect human entry into the divine world, enabling us to fully please God. He is the dream and the embodied hope of the world and the divine rest. Thus, this eternal Christ has become our holy calendar. No wonder that Christians celebrate rest on his resurrection day, as it is the day of rest on which he became the firstborn over the new creation. He opened the gates of the kingdom of God so that justice rolls down like a river and the sun of righteousness shines.

We enter the Sabbath through his resurrection which has become the seed of the new creation that spreads, turning the world of death into life and hardships into rest. Thus, Sunday is now our Sabbath; through Jesus's resurrection, we enter the world of rest. In other words, Christ rose on Sunday, the first day of the week. He turned it into a Sabbath.

On the first day of the week, Christ appeared to Mary and turned her sadness into joy (20:1–18). Also on the first day of the week, Christ appeared to the disciples (excluding Thomas). He granted them peace and commissioned them to spread it to the rest of the world (20:19–23). Later, also on the first day of the week, he appeared again.[7] Jesus, who rose from the dead, appeared to Thomas and the rest of the disciples (20:26). The good shepherd, who restored the lost sheep, turned Thomas into a believer. He said to Thomas, who doubted

---

6. Carson, *Gospel According to John*, 253.

7. Beasley-Murray, *John*, 385.

his resurrection, "Put your finger here; see my hands. Reach out your hand and put it into my side. Stop doubting and believe" (20:27). In short, our rest is in Christ, and he is our Sabbath throughout the ages. John has reread holy time in light of the coming of the Christ. In the next chapter, we will address John 6–8 in which the exodus and the wilderness traditions are also reread in light of the coming of Christ.

Discussion Questions

1. What is your culture's relationship to holy time? Are there specific days in the year or the week that are considered sacred?

2. If Christ came as the fulfillment of the Sabbath – bringing restoration, rest, and celebration into our everyday lives – how should that impact your community's engagement with holy time? Should no days be considered sacred? Should *all* days?

3. What role does the Sabbath play in your own life? How, and when, do you observe it? Would you characterize it as a time when you reorient yourself around the centrality of God and recommit yourself to live accordingly? What does that look like in your own life?

4. To what degree have you experienced the Sabbath that Christ came to bring? The healing, salvation, redemption, and rest? Can you think of specific moments in your life when you experienced some (or all) of these manifestations of the messianic age? If not, can you ask Christ to bring the fullness of the Sabbath into your life?

5. Taken as a sign, what is Jesus's healing on the Sabbath a sign of? What does it point to – and what should our response be?

5

Holy History

After challenging the teachings of water purification and the role of the temple in Pharisaic Judaism in chapter 2, and rereading the concept of the Sabbath in chapter 5, the beloved disciple considers holy history in light of the centrality of Christ.[1] Rereading the exodus and wilderness traditions, John declares that Jesus is the new Moses. From this perspective, the words of Deuteronomy are fulfilled: "The Lord your God will raise up for you a prophet like me from among you, from your fellow Israelites. You must listen to him" (Deut 18:15). Several scholars have already pointed out the similarities between Jesus in the Gospel of John and Moses.[2]

I shall mention a few of these similarities. First, both men were rejected by their own people. The book of Exodus informs us that Moses tried to help a fellow Israelite, but he was told, "Who made you ruler and judge over us?" (Exod 2:11–14). The same group of people complained against Moses several times (15:24; 16:3; 17:2). Even the people closest to him conspired against him; his own brother and sister criticized him (Num 12:1–16). Similarly, Jesus "came to that which was his own, but his own did not receive him" (John 1:11), and even "his own brothers did not believe in him" (7:5).

Second, both Moses and Christ have an association with a serpent (Exod 4:4; John 3:14). When God called Moses, he asked him to throw down his staff and it turned into a serpent. Then, when Moses stretched out his hand and held it by its tail, it turned back into a staff (Exod 4:1–4). God told Moses that when he threw it down and it turned into a serpent, the Egyptians would believe that God had called him to bring the children of Israel out of Egypt. No doubt this miraculous sign increased Moses's credibility.

---

1. Every history is biased. Every historiography is shaped by the historian's political, social, religious, economic, and cultural contexts. John is looking at history from a particular christological lens.

2. Enz, "Book of Exodus," 209.

37

Furthermore, the book of Numbers recounts the story of the bronze snake (Num 21:4–9). When the people complained against Moses, God punished them by sending venomous snakes that bit them. Then the children of Israel came to Moses asking him to intercede on their behalf so that God would have mercy on them. Moses prayed to the Lord and was instructed to make a snake and to put it on a pole: "Then when anyone was bitten by a snake and looked at the bronze snake, they lived" (Num 21:9).

Jesus likened the lifting of the bronze snake and the healing of the bitten people to him being lifted up on the cross in order to heal the world from the epidemic of sin. He said, "Just as Moses lifted up the snake in the wilderness, so the Son of Man must be lifted up, that everyone who believes may have eternal life in him. For God so loved the world that he gave his one and only Son, that whoever believes in him shall not perish but have eternal life" (John 3:14–16).[3]

Third, both the Gospel of John and the book of Exodus are structured around a series of signs and both books mention hardness of heart. Pharaoh, for example, hardened his heart more than once despite all the signs that Moses performed in front of him. God hardened Pharaoh's heart in order to reveal his incomparable power. Similarly, we encounter in the Gospel of John a set of signs as well as hardness of heart that is similar to Pharaoh's.

The Jews of the Gospel of John wanted to kill Jesus because (1) he healed on the Sabbath (5:16); (2) he said that God was his Father (5:18); (3) he was the messenger of God who, unlike other Jews, knew God (7:28–30); (4) he was the "I Am" before Abraham was (8:58); (5) he was one with the Father (10:38–39); and (6) he was doing many signs, including raising Lazarus from the dead (11:53). John's Gospel declares, "Even after Jesus had performed so many signs in their presence, they still would not believe in him. This was to fulfill the word of Isaiah the prophet. . . . He has blinded their eyes and hardened their hearts" (12:37–40).

Fourth, both Moses and Christ interceded in prayer for others (Exod 32–33; John 17). Moses interceded on behalf of Israel: when the Lord's wrath burned against Israel and he wanted to exterminate them, Moses pleaded with the Lord and his intercession changed the destiny of the children of Israel (Exod 32–33). Similarly, we encounter the intercessory prayer of Jesus only in the Gospel of John: Jesus prays for his disciples and for all those who believe through them (17:20).

---

3. The similarities are not between Christ and the serpent but in the healing that is found when the serpent is lifted up and the redemption Christ offers us through his death. For further information, see Joines, "Bronze Serpent."

Indeed, there are many similarities between Jesus, as portrayed in John, and Moses.[4] Both men are associated with manna (John 6:35; Exod 16:4, 15) and with light (John 8:12; Exod 13:21–22; 14:20). Perhaps some scholars have exaggerated the similarities between these two pertinent figures. Nevertheless, they are right in highlighting some similarities, not only between Moses and Jesus, but also between the book of Exodus and the Gospel of John, especially John 6–8. Jesus is referred to as the bread in chapter 6, the source of water in chapter 7, and the light in chapter 8. From John's perspective, he is not only the center of the Passover but is also the center of the wilderness experience. We shall unpack this point below.

There are at least four aspects of the Passover it is important to remember when considering the significance of the Passover in the Gospel of John. First, God saved Israel from death when he passed over all the homes that were marked with the blood of the lamb. The Bible says,

> On that same night I will pass through Egypt and strike down every firstborn of both people and animals, and I will bring judgment on all the gods of Egypt. I am the Lord. The blood will be a sign for you on the houses where you are, and when I see the blood, I will pass over you. No destructive plague will touch you when I strike Egypt. (Exod 12:12–13)

Second, God is holy and hates evil. Therefore, Israel should rid itself of all yeast. The Bible elaborates on this point saying, "For seven days you are to eat bread made without yeast. On the first day remove the yeast from your houses, for whoever eats anything with yeast in it from the first day through the seventh must be cut off from Israel" (Exod 12:15). Yeast is a symbol of evil (1 Cor 5:6–8). Third, the Passover is the beginning of a new calendar in which God grants life. Fourth, the Passover is a feast celebrating freedom from slavery.

John mentions the Passover (6:4) and connects it to the wilderness experiences (6:31). At the same time, he states that Jesus is the Passover Lamb (6:53–58), as well as the true manna or the bread that comes down from heaven. The Passover is near when Jesus sees a large crowd approaching him and asks Philip about feeding them. Philip estimates that bread alone would cost two hundred denarii – one denarius being equivalent to the wages of a worker for one full day.

---

4. Although Jesus is like Moses in many ways, John presents him as greater than Moses. This is also compatible with the book of Hebrews that states, "Jesus has been found worthy of greater honor than Moses" (Heb 3:3).

In the Gospel of John, Philip is usually associated with sight. For example, Philip answers Nathanael, who underestimates the significance of Nazareth and its inhabitants, by saying: "come and see" (1:46). Also, some Greeks come to Philip and say, "We want to see Jesus" (12:21). Philip dialogues with Jesus saying, "Lord, show us the Father and that will be enough for us" (14:8). Finally, when Philip looks at the crowds, he knows that he does not have enough food. But there is a boy with five loaves of barley (the food of the poor) and two fish. Jesus asks the crowds to sit on the green grass in order to show them the work of God. More than five thousand men were present. Perhaps this is the size of the army that sought to make Jesus a king (6:15). If we count men, women, and children, we can estimate a crowd of more than twenty thousand people. Jesus feeds them, and, after the people have eaten as much as they want, the disciples gather the leftovers and fill twelve baskets – a number that reminds us of the twelve tribes in the wilderness who were fed on manna. In light of this sign, Jesus speaks to four groups of people: the crowds (6:25–40); the Jews (6:41–59); the disciples (6:60–65); and the twelve (6:66–71). Jesus declares to the crowds who want daily bread that he is the bread that came down from heaven to grant life to the world (6:33). He says to the Jews who claim to know of his father and mother that he is the bread that came down from heaven (6:41–42); he is the bread of life (6:48). Then he says to his imperfect disciples that his words may be difficult, but they are words that lead to life. To Peter, one of the twelve, he declares that he is the Messiah.

Emphatically, John is rereading the history of Israel, especially the exodus and wilderness traditions, by relating them to Christ. He argues that Jesus is the bread and the source of water. As the source of water, we are reminded that when Israel was in the wilderness, God provided them with water from the rock. The association with the wilderness tradition becomes stronger when John declares that Jesus is the light. Israel was led out of Egypt into the wilderness where they received manna, drank water from the rock, and were guided by a pillar of fire. John not only connects us to Moses, the manna, and the wilderness, but he also rereads these traditions, declaring that Jesus is the bread, the source of water, and the light. The Jesus of John's gospel says, "Very truly I tell you, it is not Moses who has given you the bread from heaven, but it is my Father who gives you the true bread from heaven. . . . I am the bread of life" (6:32–35).

On the last and greatest day of the festival, Jesus says, "Let anyone who is thirsty come to me and drink" (7:37). Jesus shares these words on the day of a particular temple ritual: a priest led a procession from the pool of Siloam to the temple, and the worshippers in the procession carried a utensil filled with water. The priests blew their trumpets when the procession reached the temple's altar. They sang psalms 113–118.[5] While they were singing psalm 118, the worshippers shook the palm branches in their right hands, carrying citrus fruits in their left hands. The crowd shouted three times "Give thanks to the Lord" and then poured out the water before the Lord. First-century Jews understood that these rituals pointed to God's provision of water in the wilderness, as well as to the advent of the messianic age in which God would pour out his spirit.[6] It is in this context that Christ affirms that he is the source of water that quenches thirst. Furthermore, Jesus says, "I am the light of the world" (8:12). This statement is made in the context of a festival in which four large menorahs located in the women's court of the temple were lit.[7] In the same festival, the men danced while carrying torches. The light not only filled the temple but all of Jerusalem. In this context, Jesus states that he is the light not of Jerusalem only but of the whole world.

John is continually expanding his target audience. His vision is greater than Israel. Jesus is the bread of the world (6:33), the source of water to whoever is thirsty (7:37), and the light of the whole world, without exception (8:12). John sees Christ as the source of life regardless of where people are located, whether in Egypt, in the wilderness, or in the promised land. Israel's experiences have deeper significance in Christ. This kind of rereading comes to a crisis when Jesus discusses Abrahamic membership. After John's discussion of purification, the temple, the Sabbath, and holy history, he addresses the identity of the chosen people in chapter 8. John wants us to read Abraham in relation to Christ.

---

5. Cf. m. Sukkah 4.9. For further information, see "Mishnah Sukkah 4," Sefaria, https://www.sefaria.org/Mishnah_Sukkah.4?lang=bi.

6. Carson, *Gospel According to John*, 321–322.

7. Carson, 337.

Discussion Questions

1. In Jewish history, Moses was the ultimate leader and savior, while the exodus was the ultimate sign of God's presence, and grace, in the life of his people. What tangible signs are there of God's presence and grace in the history of your own people, your own nation?

2. Many of the metaphors for Christ are drawn from Israel's desert history – both the exodus narrative and the reality of living in a hot, dry climate. If Christ had come to your neighborhood, rather than to first-century Palestine, what metaphors might he have used to describe who he was in the world and what he had to offer?

3. How does comparison with the exodus narrative deepen our understanding of what it means for Jesus to be the bread, the water, and the light?

4. In your own life, which of these images for Christ – the bread of life (John 6:26–35), the source of living water (John 4:7–15; 7:37–38), the light of the world (1:4–9; 8:12) – most speaks to you at the moment? Why?

5. Have you ever thought of Jesus as a type of Moses? Or of Moses as a precursor, a pointer, to Jesus? Does such a comparison impact your thinking about either or both of them?

6

The Holy Nation

We encounter several major stages of the fall of humanity in Genesis 1–11. First, Adam and Eve disobey God (3:1–19). Second, Cain kills his brother Abel and Lamech kills another man (4:1–24; 4:23–24). Third, the people disobey God during the times of Noah (6:1–8). Fourth, humanity builds the tower of Babel (11:1–9). In response, God chooses Abram to change the future of the fallen world and redeem it through his seed. God asks Abram to leave the house of his father and his tribe, promising to make him into a great nation and to make his name great. God commands him, saying, "Be a blessing so that I can bless those who bless you; curse those who curse you, and that all the families of the earth can be blessed in you" (12:2–3).[1] God reveals to Abraham that his seed will be enslaved in a strange land but that God will liberate them and fulfill his purposes for the world through his seed (15:1–21). God, choosing Abraham and his seed to be a kingdom of priests and a holy nation, wants them to change the future of the world. They are expected to be a people of faith who embody liberation from sin and are to be the messengers of God to a dark, enslaved, and rebellious world. The children of Abraham have to be free in order to be messengers of divine liberation. Thus, the story of biblical Israel is intimately connected to the story of Abraham and the exodus of his children from their life of slavery in Egypt.[2]

In choosing Abraham, God also chose his seed to be rulers over God's kingdom and granted them a particular calling. The Bible says, "Israel is my firstborn son" (Exod 4:22). To be a true child of Abraham is the way towards true freedom and abundant divine blessings. Akiva (עקיבא), a famous Jewish rabbi, said that even the poorest in Israel were considered free people who lost their properties. They were free because they were the children of Abraham,

---

1. Strangely, several English translations ignore the imperative form in the Hebrew text. See Katanacho, *Land of Christ*, 36–37.

2. See Hoskins, "Freedom from Slavery."

Isaac, and Jacob.[3] Akiva was affirming that the people's connection to Abraham guaranteed their freedom, and many have assumed that Akiva was affirming the biological connection.

But Jesus challenges such perceptions as he discusses the meaning of our connection to Abraham and the God of Abraham. Jesus insists that true sonship or daughtership to Abraham is based on Abraham's faith, not his DNA. A physical connection to the seed of Abraham does not guarantee a close relationship with the God of Abraham. In fact, some of the seed of Abraham thought of killing Christ. In acting in such a way, they embodied Satan's will and desires. From John's perspective, if some first-century Jews were associated physically to Abraham, this association did not make them the children of Abraham. Unlike Abraham, they were disobeying God and obeying the devil as they sought to kill Jesus. On the other hand, Abraham believed God and obeyed him: "By faith Abraham, when called to go to a place he would later receive as his inheritance, obeyed and went, though he did not know where he was going" (Heb 11:8). By faith, he offered Isaac as a sacrifice, reasoning that God could even raise the dead (Heb 11:17–19). Christ adds, "Your father Abraham rejoiced at the thought of seeing my day; he saw it and was glad" (John 8:56).

Abraham understood that his seed would be the channel for blessing the whole world. All the nations would be blessed through him. Many Jews have agreed that Abraham possessed a spiritual insight that enabled him to see the messianic age in which God's blessings would be brought by the Messiah. But Jesus is saying more than that when he says that Abraham had seen "my day." He is claiming to be the Messiah, the Abrahamic blessing. Jesus's disagreement with many first-century Jews was not about Abraham's ability to see the future but about connecting the messianic age with Jesus of Nazareth. From John's perspective, a person could not truly accept Abraham and refuse Jesus. A Jew could not benefit from the Abrahamic blessings without Jesus Christ. John strongly affirms, "Whoever believes in the Son has eternal life, but whoever rejects the Son will not see life, for God's wrath remains on them" (3:36).

In other words, John affirms that all the Abrahamic blessings or privileges are futile without Jesus Christ. Abraham could not save people; Christ alone was the way to life. John believed that unless the children of Abraham accepted Jesus Christ, they could not see the kingdom of God. The fourth evangelist

---

3. M. B. Qam. 8:6. We can find the Hebrew quotation in the Mishnah at "14 Bava Kama 8/3–6," Sefaria, http://www.sefaria.org/sheets/48031. Following is the original Hebrew text:
משנה בבא קמא ח: ו - אמר רבי עקיבא אפילו עניים שבישראל רואין אותם כאילו הם בני חורין שירדו מנכסיהם שהם בני אברהם יצחק ויעקב.

explains this important matter with the story of Nicodemus when Jesus says to Nicodemus, "Very truly I tell you, no one can see the kingdom of God unless they are born again" (3:3).

Abraham saw the kingdom of God when he insightfully saw the day of Christ and rejoiced. John adamantly connects the true Abrahamic identity with the Messiah as he rereads the relationship with Abraham in light of the coming of the Christ. Put differently, the Abrahamic identity is larger than the Jewish identity and is not limited by DNA. No one can benefit from the Abrahamic blessings without following in the footsteps of Abraham's faith. Unfortunately, some twenty-first-century Jews and Christians have abused the idea of a physical connection to Abraham. In the name of such connections, they have justified the occupation of the Palestinian territories and the promotion of injustice.[4] They argue in the name of Abraham and God without recognizing the centrality of Jesus Christ and his inclusive love. In love, Jesus calls all people to become the children of Abraham, children of faith known by their righteous works.

In his gospel, John is interested in further identifying the followers of Christ: Who are these followers and what are their characteristics? Besides being true sons and daughters of Abraham, the followers of Christ are those who are truly free. They are the children of God, and the children of God are those who accept Jesus. John states, "Yet to all who did receive him, to those who believed in his name, he gave the right to become children of God" (1:12). They are the ones who are born of the Spirit, for flesh gives birth to flesh but the Spirit gives birth to the spirit (3:6). This community does not have to join the synagogue of the Jews (9:34). In fact, in the Gospel of John, the Jewish followers of Christ are persecuted for their faith by the majority of Jewish leaders in Jerusalem. They are persecuted and threatened with excommunication from the synagogue. John says that the Jewish leaders "had decided that anyone who acknowledged that Jesus was the Messiah would be put out of the synagogue" (9:22; 12:24; 16:2).[5] When some Jewish opponents of Christ expelled the one who was born blind from the synagogue, Christ invited him to enter the true circle of faith. As a result, the blind man worshiped him (9:35–39); he was enabled to see Christ and to believe. As a result, he became like his father Abraham, who saw Christ and rejoiced. The blind man was freed not only from physical blindness but also from spiritual blindness. He received heavenly

---

4. For further information about the biological connection to Abraham, see my *Land of Christ*, 16–26.

5. Lewis, "Preaching John 8:31–36," 179.

insight and true freedom. It might be helpful to unpack the journey towards freedom in the story of the one who was born blind.

This blind man's journey towards freedom ascended in four stages, even as the Pharisees in the same chapter descended towards bondage in four steps. John says, "Nobody has ever heard of opening the eyes of a man born blind" (9:32). We cannot find a similar story in the Old Testament or in ancient Jewish writings. Admittedly, the Old Testament speaks about opening the eyes of the blind. Isaiah informs us that a time shall come in which the blind shall see out of the gloom and darkness (Isa 29:18). On that day, the Lord shall come to save and to judge. Then the eyes of the blind will be opened (Isa 35:6). Put differently, opening the eyes of the blind was associated with the messianic, or Davidic, age in which God restores the fortunes of his people and miraculously creates new realities. Isaiah adds,

> This is what God the Lord says – the Creator of the heavens, who stretches them out, who spreads out the earth with all that springs from it, who gives breath to its people, and life to those who walk on it: I, the Lord, have called you in righteousness; I will take hold of your hand. I will keep you and will make you to be a covenant for the people and a light for the Gentiles, to open eyes that are blind, to free captives from prison and to release from the dungeon those who sit in darkness. (Isa 42:5–7)

In short, opening the eyes of the blind is a particular sign that is associated with the coming of the messianic age. No doubt first-century Jews were influenced by this background as they encountered the story of the one who was born blind. Jesus spat on the ground and made mud as if he were replicating the creation story by creating new eyes for the one who was born blind.

In any case, this messianic action initiated the journey towards freedom for this blind man. His journey was associated with his knowledge and understanding of the identity of Jesus. John's blind man describes Jesus as a man (9:10) and then argues that he is a prophet (9:17). As the Pharisees question him, he points out that Jesus is unique among the prophets, saying, "Nobody has ever heard of opening the eyes of a man born blind" (9:32). Finally, he sees the Son of Man for the first time in his life and worships him (9:35–38).

The faith journey of the man born blind is interesting. First, he understands that Jesus is a man. He says, "The man they call Jesus made some mud and put it on my eyes. He told me to go to Siloam and wash. So I went and washed, and then I could see" (9:11). Christ liberated him from physical blindness and so initiated a journey towards spiritual sight. In the midst of persecution, his insight grows stronger, and, the more he recognizes the identity of Jesus, the more he is liberated. John says, "You will know the truth, and the truth will set you free" (8:32). Second, he is liberated from begging so he could see and function differently. Third, he is liberated from enslavement to the rituals of the Sabbath and is empowered to challenge the dominant culture of rituals. Fourth, he is liberated from pleasing people in order to make financial profit. Thus, he is willing to confess Christ even if it leads to excommunication from the synagogue. Finally, he is liberated from eternal sin and condemnation. He discovers the Son of Man and worships him.

The Pharisees move in the opposite direction, towards enslavement. The more we distance ourselves from Christ, the more we become enslaved to sin. While the man born blind is ascending towards an insightful recognition of Christ, the Pharisees are descending towards spiritual blindness. Their journey towards deeper enslavement can be unpacked in several steps.

First, they are divided concerning the truthfulness of the sign of healing the man born blind (9:16). Second, they make an agreement that anyone who follows Christ will be excommunicated. For that reason, they interrogate the parents of the man born blind (9:18–23). Third, they decide that Jesus is a sinner (9:24). Fourth, while the man born blind gains physical and spiritual sight, the Pharisees, who have eyes, are declared spiritually blind. Unfortunately, they neither recognize their blindness nor seek God's help. Had they admitted that they were blind, Christ could have opened their eyes; however, they insist on resisting Christ and remain in their sin and slavery (9:39–41). Everyone who sins is a slave to sin (8:34), but the one who follows Christ shall know the truth and shall be set free (8:32).

John clarifies that Jesus is the way to freedom and develops the discussion on freedom in chapter 12. His account of Jesus's entry into occupied Jerusalem presents him as a liberating king. This is evident as the crowds are holding palm branches, which were the symbol of liberation in the Maccabean revolt. Thus, we can imagine being in the midst of a large demonstration full of provocative symbols. The crowds shout loaded statements quoted from Psalm 118:26 and cry out, "Blessed is he who comes in the name of the Lord! Blessed is the king of Israel" (John 12:13). Reflecting on Psalm 118, we observe that the expression "Blessed is the king of Israel" does not appear. But the crowds, anticipating the appearance of the kingdom of God (Luke 19:11), believed that Jesus was the king who would bring forth liberation and the kingdom of God.

They were ready to end the Roman occupation if Jesus would only agree to be their leader. Instead, as John records, Jesus entered Jerusalem riding on a donkey, which was a symbol for peace. John quotes the book of Zechariah with slight but important changes: John writes, "do not be afraid," rather than "rejoice," as in Zechariah. Following are the texts of John and Zechariah:

> Rejoice greatly, Daughter Zion! Shout, Daughter Jerusalem! See, your king comes to you, righteous and victorious, lowly and riding on a donkey, on a colt, the foal of a donkey. (Zech 9:9)

> Do not be afraid, Daughter Zion; see, your king is coming, seated on a donkey's colt. (John 12:15)

The first step towards freedom is breaking the barrier of fear by focusing on Jesus as the center of the celebration. In addition, John associates the entry of Jesus with the desire of the Greeks to see Jesus (12:21). Unlike the Synoptic Gospels, John does not address the cleansing of the temple when Jesus enters Jerusalem. Instead, he talks about the inclusion of the Greeks into the community of Jesus. How, then, should we understand the request of the Greek community?

Judas the Maccabean cleansed the temple after it had been defiled by the Gentiles in 167 BC. This Judas – not the more famous one who eventually betrayed Jesus – wanted the temple to be a place that was dedicated to God and not to idol worship. Jesus also cleansed the temple in the Synoptic Gospels, but in doing so he drove out Jews, not Gentiles, who had sinned against God and their fellow human beings. John, in his version of the entry into Jerusalem, is interested in including the nations into the community of God. He has already spoken about God loving the whole world – all those who accept Jesus regardless of their background. He has also mentioned the stories of Jesus and the Samaritan woman and Jesus and the gentile servant of the king. Then, in chapter 12, John points out the desire of the Greeks to join the community of Jesus. They want to see Jesus, perhaps just as Abraham saw him, or as the man born blind saw him and worshipped him. This does not mean mere physical sight but spiritual insight that is rooted in the recognition of Jesus as the Messiah.

Put differently, the way to achieve freedom is not the way of palm branches – that is, the militant way – nor is it the way that is rooted in an ethnocentric vision. Instead, it is the way of the grain of wheat that falls and dies in order to be transformed from an enemy into a beloved family member. The community of Christ is not an ethnic society but is open to all those who accept and advocate the way of the grain of wheat. This approach is the path towards freedom. It leads toward forming the community of Christ, the savior of the whole world, and towards understanding the unique Jewishness of Jesus.

In short, we encounter this community of Christ in its initial stages in the book of glory (chs. 13–21). In this book, Jesus calls his disciples "my children" (13:33), denoting the establishment of the messianic community, a Jewish community that follows Jesus Christ. John writes of the community of the children of Christ (13:33), the children of God (1:12), and the children of the Holy Spirit (3:5; 14:16–18). This new community of God will abide in the vine (15:1–5) and be led by the Spirit (16:13). A discussion of the identity of this new community will follow, but, first, to continue the new world order, we shall deal with the issue of the holy land as highlighted in the Gospel of John's tenth chapter.

Discussion Questions

1. As humans, we have a tendency to want to limit the grace of God to a particular group of people – usually people who look and act like us. Who are the "gentiles" of your context – the "others" who are difficult to understand, difficult to love, and difficult to imagine God accepting?

2. The blind man is liberated from enslavement to religious rituals and freed to challenge his culture and its leaders. In your own life and context, are there aspects of religious or social culture that God might be asking you to challenge? If so, what are they, and what might it look like to challenge them in Christ honoring ways?

3. What are some areas in your life in which you have experienced Christ's freedom?

4. Sight is a significant theme in this chapter. Reflect on sight/blindness in your own life. Are there areas in your life where you might need Christ to open your eyes to his perspective so you can witness his work in the world with more clarity?

7

The Holy Land

John has introduced to us the new world order which focuses on the centrality and inclusiveness of Jesus Christ. Christ is the bridegroom of the messianic age. He is the temple, the Sabbath, the center of holy history, and the focus of the chosen people. Now John addresses the concept of holy land from the perspective of the centrality of Jesus Christ.

In chapter 10, Jesus declares that he is the good shepherd and the door. In order to understand the connections between this tenth chapter and the new world order, we need to first focus on the images that are presented to us in the text. Afterwards, we will restudy the text in light of its Old Testament background, and then, we will reflect on it again in light of the sequence of ideas inside the book of John.

First, we can quickly observe that John offers seven components in his presentation. They are the door, the sheep's pen, the robber, the shepherd, the gatekeeper, the sheep, and the stranger (10:1–5). There are also seven (almost identical) components used in Christ's explanation of these images (10:7–16).

The Components of the Figure of Speech	The Components of the Interpretation
Door	Door
Sheep pen	Sheep pen
Robber	Thieves
Shepherd	Shepherd
Sheep	Sheep
Gatekeeper	Hired hand
Stranger	Wolf

Jesus is speaking about a sheep's pen in the first century. Many sheep pens were connected to caves so the sheep could shelter in the cave when it rained.

When the sun shone, the sheep would be in the court between the cave and the fence. The fence was made mainly from rocks piled up on top of each other in a way that not only prevented the sheep from escaping but also allowed the shepherd to see the sheep from outside the sheep pen. Also, the fence had an entrance, which was a door. Often, thorny plants grew over the rock wall of the sheep pen. These plants would disturb invading wolves, poking their sensitive bellies as they tried to jump over the fence. Also, if a flock of wolves surrounded the sheep pen, shepherds could light the dry, thorny plants, creating a wall of fire around the sheep. This image has a possible correlation with the book of Zechariah where it describes God's protection of Jerusalem: "And I myself will be a wall of fire around it, declares the Lord" (Zech 2:5). In other words, Jerusalem is similar to a sheep pen, and the Lord's protection is likened to a wall of fire around it.

The shepherds would bring their sheep to the pen after a long day of work. A pen could serve more than one shepherd and more than one flock, and it seems that shepherds would agree to place a guard or gatekeeper to prevent the loss of their sheep. When the shepherds returned to fetch their sheep, the gatekeeper would open the door because he recognized them. But how would they recognize their sheep? Shepherds would put certain marks on their sheep or would communicate with them with particular sounds, perhaps using a musical instrument. Some shepherds had a very intimate relationship with their sheep and named each one of them, calling them by name in order to take them to good pastures. When the sheep heard the voice of the shepherd, they knew it was time to eat, but a stranger would frighten the sheep, causing them to escape. Jesus uses this imagery and then explains it.

Christ confirms that he is the door that leads to the pen and to the good pasture. He says, "I am the gate; whoever enters through me will be saved. They will come in and go out, and find pasture" (10:9). Thus, Christ combines geography and salvation in one metaphor. Salvation is connected to the concept of entering the pen through the door and exiting with the shepherd into the good pasture. Furthermore, Christ is a door that is open to both Jews and Gentiles, for Christ has sheep that are not from the Jewish flock.[1] Salvation is also deliverance from thieves and their evil plans which entail killing and destroying the sheep. On the other hand, Christ offers a better life (10:10). The plan of God for the sheep is life, but the sheep receive life through the death of the shepherd (10:11); as the good shepherd, Christ offers himself as a substitutionary atonement. Christ is the door that restrains thieves; as the

---

1. Martin, "John 10:1-10," 172.

door, he prevents the slaughter of the sheep. He is the good shepherd who fights dangerous wolves.

Wolves spread in Palestine in the first century and lived in packs that might number from three to twenty.[2] The alpha wolf was the leader and decided when the pack should attack or retreat. The alpha wolf would try to frighten prey with certain sounds, and, when it smelled fear, it would attack, followed by the other wolves. Hired hands would run for their lives if they saw too many wolves attacking. Some shepherds would try to defend the sheep, but they would not sacrifice themselves for the sake of the sheep. Jesus, though, spoke about a good shepherd who was willing to offer himself for the sake of his sheep, delivering them from death.

With the explanation of this figure of speech in the context of the first century, it is helpful, now, to consider it in light of the Old Testament.[3] We will examine two texts from the Old Testament to help us better understand John's chapter 10.[4] The first text is from the book of Numbers: "Moses said to the Lord, 'May the Lord, the God who gives breath to all living things, appoint someone over this community to go out and come in before them, one who will lead them out and bring them in, so the Lord's people will not be like sheep without a shepherd'" (Num 27:15–17). Moses takes Joshua, son of Nun, and lays his hands on him to anoint him as the leader who will lead the people out and into the land. The book of Numbers informs us that Moses will die soon and will not enter the land. Therefore, Moses asks God to appoint a leader who will lead the people into the promised land and fight for their deliverance.

Both Joshua and Jesus carry the same name in Hebrew (יֵשׁוּעַ), are leaders, and are called shepherds. Furthermore, both Numbers and John describe these leaders with similar verbs, saying, "go in and out," a rare combination of verbs in Scripture. Perhaps this is a subtle allusion in John connecting its text to Joshua and entrance into the promised land.

However, there are also important differences between Joshua and Jesus. The former kills the inhabitants of the land in order to protect his sheep, but the latter offers himself as a sacrifice to the wolf in order to save his own. Jesus is not planning to kill the inhabitants of Palestine, but to offer himself as a substitutionary atonement. Jesus presents his description of the good shepherd at the Feast of Dedication (John 10:22). We have already spoken about the association of this feast with liberation and freedom as it is connected

---

2. Katanacho (كتناشو), أنا هو [I AM], 57–58.
3. See Kostenberger, "Jesus the Good Shepherd."
4. Carson, *Gospel According to John*, 379–390.

to the Maccabean revolt. Jesus is not only interested in the land but also in the people of the land, willing even to die in order to save them. In fact, he is the savior not only of a particular land but of the whole world. This identity drives his actions towards the people of the land. But perhaps the reader is still not convinced that John is addressing the issue of the land in relation to Jesus. Thus, it is fitting to reflect on a second Old Testament text, Ezekiel 34.[5]

Land, in John 10, is associated with the good shepherd. There are many Old Testament texts that describe God as the good shepherd. Nevertheless, one text in Ezekiel has many similarities with John 10. Furthermore, the context in Ezekiel is important. Ezekiel 33:21–37:28 begins with a discussion related to Abraham, land, inheritance, and two different perspectives. The first perspective is represented by the people who stayed in the land and insisted on their right of inheritance because of their connection to Abraham. The second perspective is represented by people in exile. They related the Abrahamic promise to a godly life. Ezekiel writes about the debate between the two perspectives: "Son of man, the people living in those ruins in the land of Israel are saying Abraham was only one man, yet he possessed the land. But we are many; surely the land has been given to us as our possession" (Ezek 33:24). How can people possess the land? Abraham took the land by faith, righteousness, and building altars for God. He did not wage wars to possess the land. In fact, he was willing to allow his nephew Lot to choose any piece of land in order to maintain peace. On the other hand, Joshua occupied the land by force and by destroying his enemies.

In any case, it is clear that the people who stayed in the land insist on their right to it based on their relationship to Abraham. They consider themselves pioneers just like Abraham and want to take the land just like Abraham and not like Joshua. Their problem does not lie in their strategy but in their timing and lack of integrity.

The exiled group challenges the advocates of the Abrahamic approach saying, "Since you eat meat with the blood still in it and look to your idols and shed blood, should you then possess the land? You rely on your sword, you do detestable things, and each of you defiles his neighbor's wife. Should you then possess the land?" (Ezek 33:25–26). The first group insists on seeing land as an inheritance and as a gift, while the other group insists on seeing righteousness as a condition for receiving the land. Ezekiel continues his discussion by presenting a long chapter about bad shepherds in Israel. He says:

> Woe to you shepherds of Israel who only take care of yourselves!
> Should not shepherds take care of the flock? You eat the curds,

---

5. Wright, *Message of Ezekiel*, 273–314.

clothe yourselves with the wool and slaughter the choice animals, but you do not take care of the flock. You have not strengthened the weak or healed the sick or bound up the injured. You have not brought back the strays or searched for the lost. You have ruled them harshly and brutally. (Ezek 34:2b–4)

Therefore, the Lord decided to take care of his flock, to save it, and to end its exile. The Lord says, "I will bring them out from the nations and gather them from the countries, and I will bring them into their own land. . . . I will tend them in a good pasture" (Ezek 34:13–14a). The age of the good pasture reflects the end of geographical and spiritual exile. Put differently, in light of the abundance of evil shepherds, God decided to take care of his sheep. He is the good shepherd who shall end exile. But how will God do that? Ezekiel informs us that God shall establish a Davidic shepherd. He says, "I will place over them one shepherd, my servant David, and he will tend them; he will tend them and be their shepherd. I the Lord will be their God, and my servant David will be prince among them" (Ezek 34:23–24).

It is obvious that Ezekiel is not talking about the historical David who has been dead for hundreds of years. Instead, he is talking about the Davidic age in which Israel's dreams about justice, righteousness, and peace shall be fulfilled. The good shepherd shall unite the people of God and lead them into the land, the good pasture. God shall establish with them a covenant of peace and shall remove all the beasts from the land (Ezek 34:25). Ezekiel associates the end of geographical and spiritual exile with the dawn of the new Davidic age. He says:

> This is what the Sovereign Lord says: I will take the Israelites out of the nations where they have gone. I will gather them from all around and bring them back into their own land. I will make them one nation in the land, on the mountains of Israel. There will be one king over all of them and they will never again be two nations or be divided into two kingdoms. (Ezek 37:21–22)

Ezekiel explains that the king who would unite the people under his banner is a new Davidic figure. He says, "My servant David will be king over them, and they will all have one shepherd" (Ezek 37:24). During his leadership, exile will be terminated. Ezekiel says, "They will live in the land I gave to my servant Jacob, the land where your ancestors lived. They and their children and their children's children will live there forever, and David my servant will be their prince forever" (Ezek 37:25). The text of Ezekiel uses the expression "one shepherd," affirming that the people of God shall be one flock (Ezek 37:15–20).

Furthermore, Ezekiel associates this Davidic age with resurrection. He describes God breathing on dead bones and turning them into a living being. God says to the dry bones, "I will attach tendons to you and make flesh come upon you and cover you with skin; I will put breath in you, and you will come to life" (Ezek 37:6). The resurrection of the dry bones is described as the resurrection of the people of God. The Bible says, "Breath entered them; they came to life and stood up on their feet – a vast army" (Ezek 37:10). The language of resurrection cannot be missed. In fact, Ezekiel explicitly says, "My people, I am going to open your graves and bring you up from them; I will bring you back to the land of Israel" (Ezek 37:12). Thus, we see the following order of ideas and images in Ezekiel's prophecy: Abraham, the good shepherd, good pasture, a united flock, and resurrection.

After studying the text of John 10 in its sociohistorical first-century context, and in relation to its Old Testament context, it is now fitting to consider it again in light of its biblical context. More specifically, I am interested in reading John 10 as part of the argument that John is presenting in the book of signs (chs. 1–12). We have already argued that John is presenting a new world order in which the major components of Pharisaic Judaism are reread in light of the centrality of Jesus Christ. In this light, John has addressed the issues of holy space, holy time, holy history, and holy people. In John 10 he is rereading holy land.

After the people went to the wilderness (chs. 6–8), it is now expected that they will enter the holy land. John adopts the scheme of Ezekiel and the order of its arguments that are related to the good pasture. Like Ezekiel, he starts by discussing Abraham (ch. 8). Then he mentions giving sight to the man born blind (ch. 9). Next, he presents his teaching about the good shepherd. Finally, John speaks of a dead person raised from his grave. We encounter not only similar themes as those in Ezekiel but also a similar order to those themes, as well as similar expressions such as "good shepherd" and "one flock."

In short, Jesus is claiming that he is the embodiment or fulfillment of the good shepherd prophecy. He not only takes care of his sheep but lays down his life to protect them from the thief who seeks to destroy them. Jesus is unlike other shepherds or hired hands. They either escape or choose their best interests over the sheep. Furthermore, Jesus is the shepherd who will make the sheep one flock led by one shepherd. He is the seed of David who embodies the covenant of peace. Under his wings, sheep can live the better life in peace, and they will not perish. Jesus offers himself as a sacrifice to save the life of the sheep and to fulfill the Abrahamic promises, especially the ones related to the good pasture or the holy land. Jesus calls his sheep by name and leads them to the good pasture. This is similar to his action towards Lazarus as he called him out of the grave into life.

Put differently, Jesus is declaring that he is the good shepherd, and, as a result, he invites us to reflect on the issue of the holy land from a christocentric perspective. No one can enter except by going through the door. Jesus is not only the door, but he is also the way (14:6). The connections between Ezekiel and John are strengthened through the resurrection story of Lazarus and by adding a description of the coming of the Spirit in chapters 14 and 16. Obviously, the life of resurrection and the presence of the Spirit are intimately related to Jesus Christ. Through him exile will be terminated, and we shall witness the dawn of a new age. Let us now reflect in more detail about the resurrection of Lazarus and how John relates life to Christ.

Discussion Questions

1. The image of the good shepherd is drawn from a herding society. In your own context, what image might Christ have used to communicate the identity of the Messiah and the ideals of a good leader?

2. As stated above, "the age of the good pasture reflects the end of geographical and spiritual exile." The theme of exile was a familiar one for first-century Jews. In your own history, what exiles have your people endured – whether physical, spiritual, or metaphorical? What might it mean for Christ to end that exile, and bring his people into "good pasture," the promised land?

3. Read Ezekiel 34. In this passage, God (through Ezekiel) juxtaposes the good shepherd with the bad shepherd. What are the attributes of each? If Christ, as the good shepherd, is the fulfillment of this prophecy, what does that mean about the nature of Christ, his kingdom, and his people?

4. Read John 10:1–18. What does this passage reveal about the nature of Christ? What does it mean, in your own life, for Christ to be the good shepherd who lays down his life for his sheep?

5. At the end of John, as we shall see in chapter 16, Christ appoints Peter as a shepherd over his flock, giving his sheep into his care. What do these two passages (Ezek 34 and John 10) – which juxtapose the good shepherd with those who are bad shepherds/thieves – teach us about leading the people of God? What does Christ expect from leaders in his church?

8

Better Life

John associates the story of raising Lazarus with the story of Mary anointing Jesus with perfume. The Gospel reads, "Now a man named Lazarus was sick. He was from Bethany, the village of Mary and her sister Martha. (This Mary, whose brother Lazarus now lay sick, was the same one who poured perfume on the Lord and wiped his feet with her hair)" (John 11:1–2).

When we go to John 12, the text directs us back to the story of Lazarus in chapter 11. It says, "Jesus came to Bethany, where Lazarus lived, whom Jesus had raised from the dead" (12:1). Put differently, John insists on connecting chapters 11 and 12 – the story of Lazarus and the story of Mary anointing Jesus with her perfume – and thus, John wants us to read the two stories together. From John's perspective, the story of Lazarus is a sign that reveals something about Jesus and the Davidic age, the age in which people experience resurrection. It is the same age in which the eyes of the blind shall be opened.

John writes, "Could not he who opened the eyes of the blind man have kept this man from dying?" (11:37). The anticipation of the messianic age is escalating, but death is the obstacle. Can the Messiah conquer death? Jesus raises Lazarus from the dead in the context of declaring his identity as the resurrection and the life, and many believed in him. The Bible says, "Meanwhile a large crowd of Jews found out that Jesus was there and came, not only because of him but also to see Lazarus whom he had raised from the dead. So the chief priests made plans to kill Lazarus as well, for on account of him many of the Jews were going over to Jesus and believing in him" (12:9–11). No doubt it will be helpful to unpack the story of Lazarus and add a few more relevant remarks.

When Lazarus became sick, the two sisters, Mary and Martha, sent a message to Jesus, saying, "Lord, the one you love is sick" (11:3). Their messenger left Bethany when Lazarus was ill, but Lazarus died after the messenger left. Unaware that he had died, the messenger informed Jesus about the illness of Lazarus, not his death. When Jesus heard the message, he stayed in his place for two days before leaving (11:6). By the time Jesus reached Bethany, Lazarus had been dead for four days (11:17). Jews believed that the spirit roamed around the corpse for three days before it departed for its final destination. Therefore, on the fourth day, no one could bring the spirit back to the body except God himself.[1]

Nevertheless, Martha implicitly suggests that God will grant the Messiah whatever he asks, including raising a dead person who has been in the grave for four days. She says, "If you had been here, my brother would not have died. But I know that even now God will give you whatever you ask" (11:21–22). After Jesus speaks about the resurrection of Lazarus on the last day with the rest of the people of God, he surprises Martha by saying, "I am the resurrection and the life. The one who believes in me will live, even though they die" (11:25). Thus, John is rereading the meaning of resurrection and life in light of the centrality of Christ. Resurrection is personified in Christ, who is the source of life and the fountain of victory over all forms of death. Whoever believes in him will never die (11:26). Instead of waiting for the day of resurrection and the last day, the age to come appears in Christ and resurrected life is found in him.

In order to prove the claim that Jesus is not only raising Lazarus but is himself the resurrection, he decides to confront the death of Lazarus publicly. His work in raising Lazarus proves his claims that he is the resurrection and life. The raising of Lazarus from the grave is similar to what the Lord had done in the book of Ezekiel. God said, "I am going to open your graves and bring you up from them; I will bring you back to the land of Israel" (Ezek 37:12). Similarly, Christ wants the grave to be opened, and he orders the dead Lazarus to come out of his grave. We don't know the location of Lazarus's spirit, but he hears the voice of Christ and returns to his body. The separation between the living Lazarus and the dead corpse ends. Christ performs this sign to demonstrate that he is the resurrection and the life which ends all forms of death and exile.

Without doubt Lazarus died twice and was buried twice. Christ raised Lazarus, but he died again. The first resurrection of Lazarus was a sign that Christ could grant him the second resurrection as well, but the second could not happen without the death and resurrection of the Messiah. Thus, the story of Lazarus is associated with the story of Mary anointing Jesus at Bethany. Let us look more closely at this story.

Mary takes expensive perfume and anoints the feet of Jesus with her hair, a woman's glory. Judas opposes this action, claiming that it is a waste of very expensive perfume, the value of which was equivalent to the wages of one

---

1. Leviticus Rabbah 18:1.

whole year of full-time work. Yet, Mary pours the entire bottle of perfume on Jesus at one time to honor him.

Jesus sides with Mary against Judas and points out that the pouring of the perfume was part of the preparation for his death and burial. In other words, John is connecting the story of raising Lazarus with the death of Christ. In fact, raising Lazarus added another reason to get rid of Christ. The opponents of Jesus were disturbed that the raising of Lazarus was convincing some to believe in Jesus. John says, "Now the crowd that was with him when he called Lazarus from the tomb and raised him from the dead continued to spread the word. Many people, because they had heard that he had performed this sign, went out to meet him" (12:17–18). John uses the word "sign," pointing out that raising Lazarus should lead us to something else. In light of the new world order, we are convinced that John is rereading the meaning of resurrection and life in light of Christ. He is advocating that Christ is the second Adam who solves the problem of death which entered the world through the first Adam. Let us explain this point further.

Many scholars have pointed out that John 1 is similar to the beginning of the book of Genesis.[2] Jeannine Brown adds that John highlights the new creation. Jesus, for example, breathes the Holy Spirit onto his disciples (20:22) in a way that is similar to God breathing his spirit into Adam (Gen 2:7).[3]

Christ was tempted in a garden and was buried in a garden. In the Old Testament garden, Adam fell into sin. Death and curse consequently entered into our world. But in the New Testament garden, the second Adam conquered the temptations and transformed the grave into a fountain of life, life that would change the whole world. This life appeared in the incarnation of Christ and began with accepting him. John starts his Gospel and ends it by affirming acceptance of the son (1:12) and the Holy Spirit (20:22). Such acceptance is the way to life and to the new world order.

John is rereading first-century Judaism in light of the coming of the Christ. This reading does not replace the Jewish people because of the false claim that they are under a curse. In fact, it does not exclude any ethnicity. Rather, it highlights the centrality of Christ, the savior of the whole world. Christ does not reject Israel but fulfills its deepest hopes through the messianic age which is intimately connected to his incarnation, death, and resurrection. He is not excluding Jews. Indeed, his first followers are all Jewish. Instead, he is enlarging

---

2. Beasley-Murray, *John*, 380–381; Brodie, *Gospel According to John*, 569; Carson, *Gospel According to John*, 651; Kostenberger, *John*, 575; Lincoln, *Gospel According to Saint John*, 499.

3. Brown, "Creation's Renewal."

the membership of the people of God through belief in the Messiah of Israel. Now it is fitting to study the book of the hour which highlights the impact of the new world order on the identity of the followers of Christ (chs. 13–21).[4]

Discussion Questions

1. What beliefs, superstitions, or fears does your culture hold regarding death? What rituals does it practice? In that context, what is the significance – the meaning – of Christ being the resurrection and the life?

2. In Ezekiel 37:11–12, God tells Ezekiel to prophecy resurrection in response to Israel's loss of hope. In the political, economic, and spiritual reality of your own nation, are there areas that feel like a valley of dry bones – lifeless, hopeless, and filled with decay? If so, what might God be wanting to communicate to you through Ezekiel 37 and John 11? What might it mean for Christ to be "the resurrection and the life" in your society, community, and culture at this moment? Where does your nation need to experience resurrection?

3. Taken as a sign, what does the resurrection of Lazarus point to? What does it indicate about the nature of Christ and his kingdom?

4. Read John 11:1–12:8, paying close attention to all references that hint at the coming death of the Messiah. Why does John link the death and resurrection of Lazarus to the coming death and burial of Jesus? What is the significance?

---

4. The expression "book of glory" or "book of the hour" is used by many commentators. For further discussion, see Brown and Moloney, *Introduction to the Gospel*, 307–315.

9

An Introduction to the Book of the Hour

After discussing the centrality of Christ in the new world order in the book of signs (chs. 1–12), it is fitting to reflect on the book of the hour (chs. 13–21), which is also called the book of glory. The literary unit begins with the words, "It was just before the Passover Festival. Jesus knew that the hour had come for him to leave this world and go to the Father. Having loved his own who were in the world, he loved them to the end" (13:1). "The hour" denotes the crucifixion of Christ, his death, and glorification. We have already discussed the meaning of the hour when we explained the sign of the wedding at Cana in the second chapter. Furthermore, the book of signs starts with the incarnation/enhumanization and ends with a glimpse of the resurrection (enacted through Lazarus). In this way, it is similar to the book of the hour. The latter book starts with the humility of Christ, which is related to his incarnation. Christ is the person who, by serving others, grants them an inheritance in the kingdom of God (13:8). The book of the hour ends with the death and resurrection of Christ (chs. 18–21).

Book of Signs (John 1–12)	Book of the Hour (John 13–21)
It starts with the incarnation (John 1).	It starts with the humility of Christ (John 13).
It ends with the death and resurrection of Christ (John 11–12).	It ends with the death and resurrection of Christ (John 18–21).

The book of signs begins with the words: "The Word became human and built his tent amongst us."[1] It ends with a discussion of burial perfume (12:7) and the kernel of wheat that must die before producing many seeds (12:24). On the other hand, the book of the hour reveals Jesus as a servant whose service is indispensable for receiving a part, or inheritance, in Christ. Jesus says to Peter, "Unless I wash you, you have no part in me" (13:8). The book of the hour ends with the death, burial, and resurrection of Jesus Christ. In this latter book, the identity of the followers of Christ is highlighted.

The book of the hour highlights seven identities within the framework of the mission of God, which starts in John with the incarnation and ends with the resurrection. I have struggled to decide whether to note seven identities or eight identities. The eighth one is the missional identity, but I have come to the conclusion that the missional identity provides the overall framework for the other seven identities. These seven identities are (1) the people of love (ch. 13), (2) the persecuted people (chs. 14, 17), (3) the people of the Spirit (chs. 14, 16), (4) the people of the vine (ch. 15), (5) the people of unity/prayer (ch. 17), (6) the people of the cross (chs. 18–19), and (7) the people of resurrection (chs. 20–21). The word "people," here, is not referring to a mere collection of human beings. I use it to refer to a group of individuals with close relationships, convictions, values, common goals, and mission.[2] It is a society created by God and sacrificial love. The individual is actively seeking to pursue the best interests of the community of Christ even if he or she loses everything for its sake.

We discussed earlier how John rereads the Old Testament, highlighting the centrality of Christ. Now, in the book of the hour, John defines the meaning of the people of God in relation to the crucified Christ who died and rose from the dead. John affirms that Jesus was a Jew. Jesus came to his own, but they did not receive him (1:11). Jesus also informed the Samaritan woman that salvation came from the Jews (4:22). His disciples were also Jewish. Pilate understood that Jesus was a Jew and said to him, "Am I a Jew? . . . Your own people and chief priests handed you over to me. What is it you have done?" (18:35). When Jesus was crucified, Pilate put a notice on the cross that read, "Jesus of Nazareth, the King of the Jews" (19:19).

---

1. The word flesh, in 1:14, denotes a human being. The context, especially verse 13, points out that being born from the flesh is being born of natural descent. Flesh in the original Greek in verse 13 refers to a human being. Thus, when we say that Jesus became flesh, we are not saying that he did not have a human soul and a spirit. On the contrary, the contextual meaning is clearly saying that he is fully human. Thus, it is better to translate 1:14 as "the Word became human" instead of "the Word became flesh." The Arabic Jesuit translation rightly prefers to translate the word *sarx* as human, while the Arabic Van Dyke translation uses the word flesh.

2. For further information see Busters (بسترس), مدخل إلى اللاهوت الأدبي [Introduction to literary theology], 24.

In short, Jesus didn't replace Judaism with Christianity. Instead, biblical Judaism was embodied and fulfilled in Christ. Jesus is the Messiah whom many generations longed for and in whom the promises of the Old Testament were fulfilled. Without him, Israel could do nothing (15:5). Without him, Israel would become like a fruitless branch that would be cast out (15:6). John divided Judaism into two kinds: the Judaism of life and the Judaism of death. The first brings forth living fruit but the latter, death. John declares, "Whoever believes in the Son has eternal life, but whoever rejects the Son will not see life, for God's wrath remains on them" (3:36).

Put differently, Jesus is the son of Adam, the son of Abraham, the son of David, and he is the new Moses. He is the perfect, sinless, and ideal Jew who makes biblical Judaism a blessing to all nations. This Judaism is not the narrow-minded first-century Pharisaic Judaism presented in John, but the Judaism of the holistic Christ, which embraces God through the holiness of Christ and embraces the whole world through the love of God. The Judaism of Christ becomes a bridge to re-create Israel. God's plan for biblical Israel is Christ. He alone is the way, the truth, and the life. Just as God breathed into dust and turned it into the living Adam, Christ breathed on his disciples and they received the Holy Spirit. Just as God called Israel his firstborn son (Exod 4:22), Christ called his disciples "my children" (John 13:33). Christ is Israel and his children are the tribes. The children of Christ are the new people of Israel. These disciples were Jewish, not Christian. They were the chosen and faithful remnant in whom the promises were fulfilled because they believed in Christ.

Many have struggled throughout history to define the relationship between Old Testament Israel and New Testament Israel. This discussion has serious implications for the relationship between Christians and Jews. Are the Jews still the people of God? Do we have two peoples of God, one Jewish and another Christian? Is the covenant with Old Testament Israel in continuity with rabbinic Judaism? How do we understand the fulfillment of the promises that were addressed to Old Testament Israel? Were these promises fulfilled in Christ or are they going to be fulfilled with the modern Jewish people? Admittedly, these questions are important. Nevertheless, Christians have strong disagreements regarding the answers to these questions. We should be careful not to impose on John our contemporary questions. He is simply speaking as a first-century Jew who discovered Christ – the Christ whom his people had been anticipating for generations. John is not speaking as a Christian who is dialoguing with Jews. He is, in fact, a Jew.[3]

---

3. For further discussion, see Brand, *Perspectives on Israel*; Katanacho, review of *Perspectives on Israel*.

Just as the New Testament does not annul the Old Testament, it does not cancel biblical old Israel but rather transforms its remnant into new Israel in light of the centrality of Christ. We can no longer understand the Old Testament without the New. Similarly, we cannot understand Old Testament biblical Israel without the new Israel. The first-century Jewish disciples of Christ are part of Old Testament Israel, but, through their relationship with Christ, they have become one with all those who believe in Christ, the New Testament Israel. They are the people of Christ. In Old Testament Israel, we have seen love, persecution, and the presence of God. We have also read about Old Testament Israel as the vine. We have encountered the exile of Old Testament Israel, the destruction of the temple, and the end of exile, which is depicted as the end of death and the beginning of resurrection. These components shaped the identity of Old Testament Israel. John rereads these same elements in light of Christ. This rereading brought forth the New Testament Israel, depicted in seven overarching identities in the book of the hour. These identities must be read within the framework of the mission of God and his people. The first identity is the people of love. We shall now unpack this identity as John describes it in chapter 13.

Discussion Questions

1. John differentiates between the Judaism of life and the Judaism of death. In your own context, are there aspects of your religious or cultural identity that bring forth life – that bring forth fruit in keeping with the teachings of Christ – and aspects that bring forth death? If so, what are they, and what differentiates the two?

2. Jesus's disciples were Jewish followers of Christ. Jesus did not come to abolish their culture but to fulfill it. What does it mean to be a follower of Christ from your own cultural and ethnic background? What does it look like?

3. Read John 13:1–17. How does this set the stage for an understanding of who Christ's followers are called to be as the people of God?

4. The book of signs ends with Jesus predicting his death. How does this set the stage for how the book of the hour begins?

5. How are the concepts of Christ's humility, enhumanization, and death connected?

10

The People of Love

Christ lived in the Roman Empire and under its occupation. He was in a country that was marked by many revolutions, wars, and dissensions. Political, religious, and social violence spread throughout the whole country. How should people have responded to such a violent environment? How could they have followed the God of Israel in such a context?

We are aware of five different responses. First, the zealots decided to respond with violence; they adopted "an eye for an eye" mentality and engaged in violent military resistance. Judas the Galilean established this sect during the days of the census of governor Quirinius (see Acts 5:37). The Roman governor Quirinius sought to increase taxation, but the zealots resisted his policy.[1] Their leader, Judas, provoked the people of Judah to initiate a military revolt against the Romans. It seems that Simon the Zealot belonged to this sect, yet he became a disciple of Jesus (Luke 6:15; Acts 1:13). Perhaps, like other zealots, he used to see every stranger as an enemy. But who was the stranger in the ideology of zealots? The stranger was any person who was different religiously or ethnically. The stranger was the one who did not adopt the same values and customs that a zealot advocated.

Second, the Pharisees were strongly committed to the Mosaic Torah. They fought against Hellenization, the integration of Greek civilization with Jewish culture.[2] They insisted that truth and justice were found in the Mosaic Torah. The Torah was the best answer to the problems of life, and, furthermore, the oral tradition was the best way to understand the Torah. The Pharisees separated themselves from the nations and considered them defiled. When they reflected on the *Lex Talionis*, the law of an eye for an eye, they were willing to

---

1. Josephus, *Wars of the Jews*, 2.8.1. See also Josephus, *Antiquities of the Jews*, 18.1.6.

2. Some of the Pharisaic leaders knew Greek and were influenced by Hellenistic civilization, but their official stance was to stand against Hellenization. For further details, see Hengel, *Hellenization of Judaea*, 37.

abandon the literal interpretation if the attacker was willing to pay a financial fine. This is similar to a traditional Palestinian cultural solution (still in effect) known as *sulha*. In *sulha*, an attacker who injures a victim may offer financial compensation for the injury.

Third, the Sadducees tried to bridge their faith and the Hellenistic context. The Sadducees were an aristocratic group who controlled the temple and dealt with the ruling Romans. They represented the Jews in addressing political issues before the Romans. They saw Roman authority as an imposed political partner; thus, they sought to coexist and adopted a pragmatic political agenda, intending to achieve maximum gain with minimum sacrifice.

Fourth, the Essenes decided to distance themselves from Jerusalem. They shunned the temple, other Jewish sects, and interaction with the Romans. The Essenes were committed to the hatred of evildoers and the love of truth.

Fifth, Christ came with a different approach. He spoke about loving the enemy and acted with love towards those who mistreated him. For example, he forgave Peter who denied him and washed the feet of Judas who betrayed him. His life became a model for all who followed him. Thus, he created a new group, the people of love, with a different approach. This group was "his own" (13:1), his disciples (13:5), the clean ones (13:10), and the chosen ones (13:18). He considered them his children, addressing them as, "My children" (13:33). It seems strange to call someone who is older than you "my child," but Christ was their spiritual parent. He was the mother of a new people who would embody eschatological Judaism and the father of the New Israel. Membership in his family was intimately related to the glorification of the Father in the Son, to the death and resurrection of Jesus Christ. He had to go to the cross (13:33) because there he would embody the best kind of love. Let us look closer at this love.

There is no doubt that John is interested in the motif of love, especially in chapter 13. The chapter starts with the following statement: "Having loved his own who were in the world, he loved them to the end" (13:1). The expression "to the end" denotes that he loved them all of his life until his last breath. It could also mean that he loved them with all of his heart. It is 100 percent love in terms of time and quality. John is declaring that love is foundational in the relationship between Christ and his followers. It is, in fact, an indispensable part of his followers' identity and the marker that makes them known. Christ says, "By this everyone will know that you are my disciples, if you love one another" (13:35).

Furthermore, in chapter 13, we encounter the betrayal of Judas (13:18–29) and the denial of Peter (13:36–38). Sandwiched between these two texts we find Christ's commandment: "A new command I give you: Love one another. As I have loved you, so you must love one another" (13:34). Christ did not give this commandment when things were going well. In fact, his commandment appears in a very awkward but deliberate place, sandwiched between betrayal and denial. We must be committed to love even when the ones we love fail us. This encourages us to reflect more closely on the way that Christ loved his disciples. How did he love them?

A few days before his crucifixion, Jesus poured some water in a basin and washed the feet of his disciples (13:5). He loved them despite their dirty feet and their many other shortcomings. He expressed his love in practical ways. Since first-century Palestinian roads were dusty with all kinds of dirt, the disciples' feet were dirty, but Jesus washed them as an act of love that required a great deal of humility. This picture of humble love, which depicts the lover as a slave washing the feet of others, is shocking. But, perhaps, it is less shocking than the humble love that motivated God himself to become a human being who washes away our sins. Christ served like a slave, washing the feet of the disciples. Foot washing was the humblest job, which only certain kinds of slaves had to do. Perhaps some disciples would have agreed to wash the feet of their master, Jesus Christ, but it is amazing that Christ himself, their master, washed their feet. This amazement is even stronger in light of John's declaration, "Jesus knew that the Father had put all things under his power, and that he had come from God and was returning to God," yet he got up and washed the feet of his disciples (13:3–4). Some Jews insisted that only Gentile slaves, women or children could perform the task of foot washing; a Jewish male slave should not be asked to perform such a demeaning task.

The disciples not only had dirty feet, but they also had cognitive issues. The master loved them despite their lack of understanding. Love does not endorse ignorance or stupidity. Nevertheless, it is patient and hopeful as it anticipates the time in which cloudiness is dispelled. Let us illustrate this point from the life of Peter. Peter did not understand the plan of God or the plan of the cross, and he was not fully aware of the methods God uses to accomplish his will. Thus, Christ said to him, "You do not realize now what I am doing, but later you will understand" (13:7). Peter did not understand the actions of Christ. Thus, Jesus asked him to postpone his evaluation of such actions. He would understand them after the cross, the resurrection, the ascension, and Pentecost.

Perhaps Peter could not understand then, but he would understand later. Peter, though, insisted on doing things in his own time and his own way. Thus, Christ said to him, "Where I am going, you cannot come" (13:33). Peter said, "Lord, why can't I follow you now?" (13:37). Christ assured him that although he could not follow him then, he would follow him later (13:36). Christ shows us that true love does not endorse ignorance but is patiently working to spread truth. Christ removed the dirt from the feet of the disciples, and he would also clean their hearts and minds and diminish their misunderstanding through his sacrificial love. This is the same love that led to his sacrificial death on the cross.

John says that Christ knew that the hour of his death had come (13:1) and that the Father had given everything into his hands (13:3). Peter did not listen to the evaluation of Christ who said to him, "You do not realize now what I am doing, but later you will understand" (13:7). Peter's ignorance lasted for a long time. Even after the resurrection of Christ, his appearances to the disciples, his ascension into heaven, and Pentecost, Peter did not understand the vision of Christ that led him to humble himself and act as a slave. Peter's lack of understanding deteriorated into a ground zero mentality, a narrow-minded perspective that sees things only from one side and then decides what is right and wrong without considering the different options properly. Peter insisted on keeping his position and his cultural standards. How could he violate the expectations of his culture? Peter did not consider the option chosen by Christ because he was not willing to reflect on countercultural possibilities. But God, continuing to have mercy on Peter, showed him a vision explaining that what God cleanses no human being should consider unclean (Acts 10:9–16). The Bible says that Peter "saw heaven opened and something like a large sheet being let down to earth by its four corners. It contained all kinds of four-footed animals, as well as reptiles and birds. Then a voice told him, 'Get up, Peter. Kill and eat'" (Acts 10:11–13). Peter did not accept God's invitation to eat, so God spoke to him again (Acts 10:15). Peter's journey towards a mature understanding took much time, but he understood eventually.

During this journey, Christ showed Peter a lot of tough love, the kind of love that does not compromise divine truth. Jesus said to Peter, "Unless I wash you, you have no part with me" (John 13:8). This was not a threat but an explanation of the results of Peter's decision that Christ would never ever wash his feet. The word "part" can also be understood as inheritance. Thus, it is possible to understand that Christ was telling Peter that unless he washed his feet, he would have no inheritance among his people. Peter was moved by Christ's insistence on acting as a slave in order to offer this inheritance to his followers, but he still did not understand the full implication of the words of Christ. He then asked Christ not only to wash his feet, but also his hands and head, hoping that he would become cleansed and acceptable before God; however, Christ clarified that God's pleasure is not found in bodily cleansing or rituals but in loving hearts. Although Peter's perception was shallow, Christ used the opportunity to further clarify his intentions.

The love of Christ not only leads to a better understanding of the will of God but also embodies right behavior. Jesus said to his disciples:

> Do you understand what I have done for you? . . . You call me "Teacher" and "Lord," and rightly so, for that is what I am. Now that I, your Lord and Teacher, have washed your feet, you also should wash one another's feet. I have set you an example that you should do as I have done for you. (John 13:12–15)

There is no excuse for those who abandon the way of love, for Christ declared this way when the devil prompted Judas to betray Jesus and when Jesus knew who was going to betray him (John 13:2, 11). Consequently, we can apply the role of love to the Palestinian context. How can a Palestinian Christian citizen of Israel embody the love of Christ?

The love of Christ was seen in the accounts of the betrayal of Judas and the denial of Peter. Other stories of betrayal in the Bible include the following: the rebellion of Aaron and Miriam against their brother Moses (Num 12:1–11); the betrayal of Moses by Korah (Num 16:1–33); the betrayal of King Asa by Zimri (1 Kings 16:15–16); the betrayal of the city of Luz by one of its citizens (Judges 1:22–26); the betrayal of the Amalekites by an Egyptian lad (1 Sam 30:1–20); the betrayal of King Xerxes by Bigthana and Teresh, two of the king's officers who guarded the doorway (Esther 2:21–23); and the betrayal of David by his son Absalom (2 Sam 15:1–12).

Betrayal has been abhorred throughout history. Most countries consider it a serious crime, punishable in some nations by death. In his Divine Comedy, Dante considered it the worst kind of sin, putting those who committed it in the lowest and worst parts of hell.[3] A traitor usually helps the side opposing his or her own group, even if the betrayal involves the shedding of blood. Betrayal in the Old Testament, or even in the first century, was not a mere political issue. It was also a religious one. To betray the king was also understood as betraying God and siding with Satan. In fact, many religious states have combined politics and religion, so that betraying one's country is equivalent to betraying God himself. Consequently, we need to consider that the betrayal of Christ by Judas was not only a personal issue, but it was also a betrayal of the kingdom of God in order to maintain the kingdom of Israel.

---

3. For further information, see Alighieri (أليجيري). الكوميديا الإلهية [The divine comedy], 403–434.

John reveals this side of the story when he explains the discussion taking place among the leaders of Jerusalem. The leaders were afraid that if the people believed in Jesus, then the Romans would come and take the temple and the nation away from them (11:48). Therefore, the high priest Caiaphas stood and said that it was better to sacrifice one man than the whole nation (11:50). He was willing to sacrifice Jesus for the sake of maintaining the rule of Jewish authorities. Thus, the betrayal of Christ was not only an embodiment of the evil of one individual, it was also a sociopolitical evil advocated in the name of maintaining the kingdom of Israel. It was recruiting religion to serve political agendas. It was an abuse of religion. The main components of the kingdom that Caiaphas had in mind were the temple, the nation, and possibly the land in which they lived. Since it seemed that Jesus was claiming to be a king and thus was dangerous, it was better to get rid of him. The Johannine Jews had tried to kill Jesus more than once, but, after he raised Lazarus from the dead, they were even more determined to execute Jesus.[4]

Ananias was the high priest during the years 15–6 BC. The Roman leader Valerius Gratus removed him from his position, and, consequently, five of his children became high priests, one after the other. Then Caiaphas, his son-in-law, became the high priest during the time of the crucifixion of Christ.[5] The high priests wanted to get rid of Jesus for religiopolitical reasons. They did not want to lose the land and their Jewish identity. Consequently, the Sanhedrin called a meeting and decided to eliminate Jesus for good. Sadly, in the name of a distorted Judaism, they not only ignored Christ but also advocated murder. After the meeting of the Sanhedrin, John records that the religious leaders were explicitly plotting to take the life of Christ (11:53). Thus, they took advantage of the weakness of Judas Iscariot, one of Christ's disciples. He loved money and did not care about the poor. He was a thief (12:6). He had an unclean heart (13:10–11). His wickedness became a nesting place for Satan who entered him and shaped his will (13:27). Consequently, he conformed to the path of murder and surrendered to the wicked schemes of Caiaphas. He wanted Jesus to be killed.

Judas is an example of a human being who surrendered to political evil and oppression instead of choosing justice. The Jewish religiopolitical authorities in Jerusalem had decided to kill an innocent. They overlooked justice and religious virtues, violating basic human rights for the sake of fulfilling their

---

4. I have used the expression "Johannine Jews" to avoid putting all the first-century Jews, as well as Jews throughout history, in one category. Jesus Christ, Peter, and most first-century followers of Christ were also Jews. But they did not follow the counsel of Caiaphas.

5. Carson, *Gospel According to John*, 580–581.

political goals. The Jewish nation was their priority. They wanted the land, the holy space. Their misguided priorities led them to ignore God's priorities. God wanted justice and love for all and to establish a new world in which Christ was at the center. They went astray because they surrendered to satanic pressures to the point of killing. Judas was a person who tried to deceive Jesus with a kiss, walked the path of evil in order to pursue economic gain, and walked the path of violence in the name of national security for first-century Jewish people.

Sadly, Judas is still alive in our midst. There are people today who advocate national ideologies that ignore justice and peace. Such ideologies also justify violence, murder, and selfish economic gain in the name of patriotism. Those who adhere to such ideologies seek to control the land even at the expense of justice and peace. Judas is not an Israeli or a Palestinian. Rather, he is any person who walks in the path of oppression. He is any government which advocates violence in the name of the country or of God. God is the judge and the one who declares who is Judas. The violations of human rights testify against anyone who adopts the worldview of Judas.

Some justify the worldview of Judas according to the apostle Paul who said, "Let everyone be subject to the governing authorities, for there is no authority except that which God has established. The authorities that exist have been established by God" (Rom 13:1). They justify state terror in the name of God and the Bible, but this interpretation is wrong and is not compatible with a biblical worldview. A quick look at Romans 13 reveals that those same authorities (to whom the people of God are to be subject) are not a threat to those who do what is right but only to those who do wrong (Romans 13:3). Put differently, a follower of Christ submits to just laws and to governors who uphold such laws. The text adds:

> Do you want to be free from fear of the one in authority? Then do what is right and you will be commended. For the one in authority is God's servant for your good. . . . [Rulers] are God's servants, agents of wrath to bring punishment on the wrongdoer. Therefore, it is necessary to submit to the authorities, not only because of possible punishment but also as a matter of conscience. (Romans 13:3–5)

However, when the ruler does not uphold justice, he or she is no longer an agent of divine wrath over wrongdoers but is an agent of oppression. In such cases, God must be obeyed even if it entails resisting the authority of rulers.

The Bible is full of examples in which people of faith, conscience, and virtue challenge governors for the sake of extending justice and the kingdom of

God. The apostles Peter and John, for example, say to the leaders of Jerusalem, "Which is right in God's eyes: to listen to you, or to him? You be the judges! As for us, we cannot help speaking about what we have seen and heard" (Acts 4:19–20). When the high priest and the Sanhedrin interrogate the apostles of Christ, seeking to prevent them from spreading truth, their answer is, "We must obey God rather than human beings" (Acts 5:29)!

Having discussed Judas and his worldview, it is fitting to reflect on Peter from a Palestinian point of view. It is evident that Peter is a central figure in the book of John. This man is known by several names, including Peter, Simon, Simon son of John, Simon Peter, and Cephas.[6] Regardless of his name, he is a loyal person who loves Christ and is even willing to die for the sake of his master.

Indeed, these are impressive claims, but Peter had to be tested to demonstrate that his actions lived up to his words. He went through a difficult test. Would he deny Christ under religious and political pressure? If he admitted his relationship to Jesus, then he would become an enemy of the Jerusalemite religious leaders as well as powerful Rome. Perhaps he would lose his head. But if he denied Jesus, he would deny his most important life discovery. He would deny himself and the calling on his life to be salt and light in a dark and fallen world. Furthermore, he would deny the way of love, loyalty, peace, and justice. He would deny human rights and adopt the path of fear. In vain, he would be seeking to save his life. He would be blinded by his selfish interests, forgetting that those who abandon truth lose everything. Peter struggled with two choices: should he declare his identity or hide it? He failed the test and even denied his own identity.

Let us reflect on Peter from the perspective of Palestinian Christian citizens of Israel. We, too, face the question of whether to hide or declare our cultural, religious, and political identities. We are Palestinians culturally, Christians in our faith, and we are also citizens of Israel. This combination presents several challenges, especially in light of the Palestinian-Israeli conflict and the rise of religious extremism in the Middle East.

Returning to Peter, he went to the house of the high priest and a female servant asked him: "You aren't one of this man's disciples too, are you?" (John 18:17). She expected a negative answer and Peter gave her a clear negative answer as he replied, "I am not" (18:17). Furthermore, Peter denied his relationship to Jesus again in the presence of servants and slaves who stood

---

6. Following is the frequency of some of this nomenclature in the Gospel of John: "Peter" occurs thirty-four times, "Simon" appears twenty-one times, "Simon son of John" occurs in four references, and "Cephas" occurs in John 1:42.

around a fire to keep warm. While he was standing with them and warming himself, they asked him, "You aren't one of his disciples too, are you?" (18:25). He denied his relationship to Christ again saying, "I am not." One of the slaves, though, argued that he had seen him with Jesus in the garden, but Peter insisted on denying Christ.

John repeats the words of Peter, "I am not," twice. In the same literary unit, we encounter the affirmation of Christ, "I am he." When the soldiers, with Judas, come to arrest Christ, he asks them, "Who is it you want?," (18:4) and then replies, "I am he" (18:5). He affirms his identity before the armed soldiers while Peter denies his identity before a slave girl. Jesus asks them again who they want and again affirms his identity. The repetition of Peter's denial twice and Christ's affirmation twice in the same literary unit leads us to compare the two responses. Peter denied Christ, his friendship, and his own identity before the least powerful of people. On the other hand, Christ affirmed his identity and friendships before the most powerful.

Peter had to deny his own Galilean accent. Matthew says, "After a little while, those standing there went up to Peter and said, 'Surely you are one of them; your accent gives you away'" (Matt 26:73). In order to deny his connection with Jesus, Peter had to deny his Galilean culture and the messianic values of integrity that Christ demanded. He resisted his core values because he was afraid. Many Palestinians in Israel act like Peter. Culturally Palestinian, and holding Israeli citizenship, these two identities are in conflict for their state is fighting their people, as well as their culture. They live in a world in which Arabic and Hebrew are in enmity with each other. They assume that these two languages represent two rival cultures, but this is not true.

When the political situation is tense, many Palestinians in Israel don't speak Arabic in stores or public places where Israeli Jews are the majority. They tend to hide their identity lest extremists attack them. Some Palestinians seek to emphasize their Israeli identity and downplay being Palestinian, walking the path of Israelization. They choose to live today even if it means the death of their identity tomorrow. Others deny their Israeli identity, fearing that they might be perceived as traitors by their own people, so they shun anything that connects them to the state of Israel. Instead, they should seek to build a just society for both Palestinians and Jews and a state for all its citizens. Unfortunately, they deny their identity rather than thanking the God who granted them a unique identity with the potential to bring glory to him. Our Palestinian cultural identity is not a sin but a blessing. Why do we deny it? Our citizenship in Israel is not treason but an opportunity to build bridges of peace and a future in which evil is defeated and ethnic diversity is celebrated. Our calling is to be good citizens of Israel and to love our Palestinian people, as well as our Jewish co-citizens. Our calling is to fight against all forms of evil and to seek all forms of good for all of our neighbors. Furthermore, we, as Christians, are responsible to care for every oppressed and afflicted person in our circles.

Denying our identity out of fear of religious extremism will not solve our problems. As we address extremism among Muslims, we should recognize that our true challenge is not our Palestinian identity but our Christian faith. Our challenge with our Jewish brothers and sisters is not their Judaism or culture but the political and social evils that hinder the building of a world of love and justice. Denying our identity will lead us to apathy and a lack of sensitivity towards our own people. But affirming our identity will lead us to self-understanding and an understanding of the call of God on each one of us, and on our nation as a whole. The way of love celebrates our God-given identities and dedicates and sanctifies them for the service and glory of God. When we deny our identities, we deny God's grace and our calling. God has gifted us with specific identities through which to honor him. When we deny those identities, we not only deny our individual identity but also our collective identity and our people. We, therefore, walk the path of hatred rather than the path of love. Let the Jew celebrate his or her Jewish identity, sanctify it, and offer it as a gift to God. Likewise, let the Palestinian celebrate his or her identity, sanctify it, and offer it to God. Let us love our complex identity, our Palestinian people, and our Israeli compatriots. Let us share our lives with them, serve them, and love them as Christ loved us. Thus, we place our Palestinian identity and our Israeli citizenship on God's altar, asking him to sanctify and use them as a blessing to all the people around us.

In short, Christ has called us to be people of love. In the next chapter we consider our second identity in the Gospel of John: we are called to be people of the Spirit.

Discussion Questions

1. As we have seen, Christ lived in a time that was politically volatile and violent. What challenges does your own community face politically, religiously, or socially? How is the church choosing to respond to those challenges? Does that response mirror the example Christ set for us in the Gospel of John? If not, how could the church more fully reflect Christ's calling to be the people of love?

2. Washing the feet of the disciples was a tangible sign of humble love in first-century Palestine. What would be an equivalent sign in your own contemporary context?

3. Christ gives his disciples their new commandment – to love one another – between Judas's betrayal and Peter's denial. What implications might this have for your own life? Are there people you believe are undeserving of love, due to their treatment of you? What might Christ say to that perspective?

4. Are there ways in which you face the temptation to deny aspects of your own identity? What would it mean to fully embrace your identity as a gift from God, to be sanctified and used for God's glory? How is God calling you to be part of the people of love, not despite your identity, but by using that identity?

11

The People of the Spirit

In the book of signs, John speaks about the Holy Spirit more than once (1:32–33; 3:5–8; 4:23–24; 6:63; 7:37–39). The following table shows these texts:

1:32–33	I saw the Spirit come down from heaven as a dove and remain on him. . . . "The man on whom you see the Spirit come down and remain is the one who will baptize you with the Holy Spirit."
3:5–8	Very truly I tell you, no one can enter the kingdom of God unless they are born of water and the Spirit. Flesh gives birth to flesh, but the Spirit gives birth to spirit . . . The wind blows wherever it pleases. You hear its sound, but you cannot tell where it comes from or where it is going. So it is with everyone born of the Spirit.
4:23–24	Yet a time is coming and has now come when the true worshipers will worship the Father in the Spirit and in truth, for they are the kind of worshipers the Father seeks. God is spirit, and his worshipers must worship in the Spirit and in truth.
6:63	The Spirit gives life; the flesh counts for nothing. The words I have spoken to you – they are full of the Spirit and life.
7:37–39	"Let anyone who is thirsty come to me and drink. Whoever believes in me, as Scripture has said, rivers of living water will flow from within them." By this he meant the Spirit, whom those who believed in him were later to receive. Up to that time the Spirit had not been given, since Jesus had not yet been glorified.

Interpreters might disagree on defining the semantic range of the word "Spirit" in these verses. Nevertheless, it is clear that, from John's perspective, the Holy Spirit leads us to discover the Son of God. John quotes the Baptist, saying, "And I myself did not know him, but the one who sent me to baptize with water told me, 'The man on whom you see the Spirit come down and remain is the one who will baptize with the Holy Spirit'" (1:33). The Spirit is the mother that grants us our new kingdom identity and enables us to see the kingdom as well as to enter it (3:5–8). The one who is born from the flesh is flesh, but the one who is born of the Spirit is spirit (3:6). The flesh cannot enter the kingdom of God or communicate with God, for God is Spirit and must be worshipped in the Spirit. The nature of God defines the nature of worship; God must be worshipped in the Spirit (4:23–24). The Spirit alone is the right means to acceptable and true worship as well as to life. St Symeon, the New Theologian (AD 949–1022), said that the Spirit is the key to the house (3:3–5), the Father is the house (14:2), and Christ is the door (10:7–9).[1]

Put differently, we cannot attain life except through the Spirit (6:63). The Spirit, the mark of the Davidic age, interprets the words of Christ in order to bring forth life in us. The Bible says that on the last and greatest day of the Festival of Tabernacles (7:2, 37), Jesus spoke about the Spirit. Usually, this festival fell in September or October, and, on the seventh day, the high priest led a procession of priests carrying gold bowls filled with water from the pool of Siloam to the temple. People enjoyed the sight of the procession, as well as the sound of blasting trumpets as the priests headed to the temple altar.[2] They sang Psalm 118 and then shouted three times: "Give thanks to the Lord!" Then they poured water and wine into silver containers before pouring it out before the Lord. First-century Jews understood that these rituals signified that God would provide the water and would pour out the Spirit in the age to come.[3]

In addition to the five references already mentioned, John provides five major sections about the Holy Spirit in his farewell discourse (14:15–21; 14:25–26; 15:26–27; 16:5–11; 16:12–16). Jesus says, "And I will ask the Father, and he will give you another advocate to help you and be with you forever" (14:16). Christ, the first comforter, loved his disciples and taught them, protected them, and guided them into truth. But he was going to leave them since he would die, be buried, and ascend into heaven. He was the father of the disciples (13:33), but when he died, they would become orphans without a guide, a leader, a comforter, or a protector. The word *Parakletos* is used to denote a person who helps the accused in court, and in 1 John 2:1, it has been translated as "advocate." The paragraphs that are related to the Holy Spirit in the book of the hour indicate the relationship of the Holy Spirit to the Trinity, the disciples, and the world.

---

1. Scouteris, "People of God," 416.
2. M. Sukkah 4:9.
3. Carson, *Gospel According to John*, 322.

First, let us examine the texts related to the relationship of the Holy Spirit and the Trinity. This topic is difficult to explain but is very important to address. Christians believe in one God who is three persons. We advocate the oneness of God without denying the distinctiveness of the Father, Son, and Holy Spirit. The one God is Father, Son, and Holy Spirit. The third person of the Trinity is called the Holy Spirit. The Spirit is the Comforter, the Spirit of Truth, and the Holy Spirit. Thus, the Holy Spirit is similar in these aspects with the second person of the Trinity, the Son. Christ is also the Comforter (14:16), the Truth (14:6), and the Holy One whom the Father sanctified (10:36). Furthermore, the Father is the Holy God (17:11), the True God (17:3), and the God of all Comfort (2 Cor 1:3).

The Father sends the Holy Spirit (John 14:26) and the Son sends the Holy Spirit (15:26; 16:7), but the Holy Spirit comes out of the Father (15:26). This procession of the Holy Spirit is how we understand the eternal relationship between the Father and the third person of the Trinity; it is before creation, whereas sending the Spirit is within creation. Stated differently, the procession of the Spirit is within the ontological Trinity – that is, referring to the Trinity in itself without regard to God's work in creation. The sending of the Holy Spirit is understood in the framework of the economic Trinity – that is, the activity of God and the role of the three persons of the Trinity regarding creation and redemption.

In addition, John affirms the relationship of the second and third persons of the Trinity, saying: "When the Advocate comes, whom I will send to you from the Father – the Spirit of truth who goes out from the Father – he will testify about me" (15:26). The Son says that the Holy Spirit "will glorify me because it is from me that he will receive what he will make known to you" (16:14). Thus, the Holy Spirit, the third person of the Trinity, leads us to the Son who leads us to the Father. The Trinity (Father, Son, and Holy Spirit) is one essence despite having different roles. Thus, we should not separate the people of the Spirit from the Trinity. Their role is associated with the Spirit who glorifies the Son and testifies about him. When the Son is glorified, then the Father is also glorified.

Second, we shall now study the relationship of the Holy Spirit to the world. John informs us that the world cannot accept the Spirit; it neither sees him nor knows him (14:17). The world represents every human being who rejects the Johannine Christ, his teachings, and his atonement. The Holy Spirit acts like the prosecutor who convicts the world. The Bible says, "When he comes, he will prove the world to be in the wrong about sin, righteousness and judgment: about sin, because people do not believe in me; about righteousness, because I am going to the Father, where you can see me no longer; and about judgment, because the prince of this world now stands condemned" (16:8–11).

The word "prove" in its original language can be interpreted in several ways: put to shame, despise, accuse, examine, test, prove, expose, rebuke, or refute. The biblical text describes three spheres in which the Spirit relates to the world: sin, righteousness, and judgment. After each sphere the text provides the grounds for proving the world to be in the wrong. It is clear that the Spirit will evaluate the world, its worldviews, concepts, feelings, behaviors, ethics, and politics, in light of the kingdom of Christ and his teachings.

The Spirit is interested in justice. Being the people of love does not mean overlooking justice. Love is not an excuse to abandon justice but an opportunity to pursue it. Thus, the people of the Spirit are people of justice and righteousness. The results of an active Spirit will demonstrate that the world is guilty and that the divine standards of holiness are higher than the best human efforts can attain. The world is guilty of its sins, standards of righteousness, and judgments. The world sins when it breaks the law of God and chooses human standards instead of divine ones. The world also sins in its satanic judgment that employs authority to accomplish the plans of the evil one. This is exactly what happened in the tribunal of Christ when the court system failed and spilled innocent blood.

Third, in light of the previous two points, we shall explain the relationship of the Spirit with the disciples, the people of the Spirit. The Spirit would be their comforter and be with them forever (14:16). He would teach them and remind them of all the things that Christ had taught them (14:26). He would guide them into all truth. The presence of the Holy Spirit, with the disciples and in them (14:16–17), transformed them into the people of the Spirit. They became the temple of God's Spirit and were distinguished from the rest of the world by their knowledge of God, not only a cognitive knowledge, but an experiential one as well. They had accepted God and had seen him through their belief in Jesus Christ.

Christ says to Philip, "Anyone who has seen me has seen the Father" (14:9). The presence of Christ leads to seeing God and knowing him. It leads to becoming the temple of God's Spirit whose activity testifies to the Son, and in this way, we know the triune God. This knowledge declares that we are no longer orphans. We have insightful eyes that can see that Christ is alive and that we live because he lives. Furthermore, the Spirit guides us into truth in a violent and oppressive world. Indeed, the words of Christ were spoken in the context of Roman occupation and political oppression. In addition, Caiaphas demonstrated the abuse of power among religious leaders.

We also encounter the hypocrisy of the crowds who cheered on Palm Sunday to welcome Christ as king but shouted on Friday to demand that Jesus be crucified. Our world is similar to the world of the disciples. We also encounter evil within individuals, communities, and states. Therefore, we need to listen to the voice of the Spirit and heed his guidance in the midst of this confusion. The Spirit guides us to Christ, who is the personal, social, and cosmic savior. He saves whoever comes to him and confesses his or her sin. Many Christians rightly highlight personal salvation, but unfortunately, they overlook other aspects of salvation. Christ, as the savior of our cultures and societies, came to overcome all forms of evil. He does not want to merely save our spirits and transport us to heaven. On the contrary, he wants to bring the kingdom of God to earth. A spiritual person is not one who shuns material things, but one who is sanctified in his or her spirit, soul, and body. A spiritual person is one who becomes a messenger of the kingdom of God here and now and whose God longs to create a just society full of righteousness, peace, and love. God desires to clone the love of Jesus in all of his disciples, all the people of the Spirit.

In light of all this, it is important for Palestinian people of the Spirit in Israel to address not only personal salvation through Christ but also the salvation of our societies. It is important for us to pursue justice in love as we seek peace. Christ is the peacemaker who provides forgiveness and reconciles us both to God and to each other. He is the lord of justice who vindicates the oppressed. The people of the Spirit must become Christ-like as they form an alternative community in a perishing world. Arab, Jewish, and other followers of Christ must work together in one body to embody the community of the Spirit in Palestine and Israel. This will not happen without declaring Christ as our center and without a full submission to the Spirit of truth and holiness. We shall not succeed without truth, justice, holiness, and love. When we obey the Spirit, we honor Christ, but it is fair to ask what kind of Christ we are honoring.

Could he be an ethnically biased Christ, a Palestinian Christ, a Jewish Christ or a denominational Christ? It seems that Christ is inclusive in his love and atonement for all who believe in him. He is the personal and cosmic Savior, the savior of our societies. Without a comprehensive and inclusive vision for all the inhabitants of Israel/Palestine, we do not advocate a just Christ. A just Christ envisions a world in which we all live together in dignity, free of bigotry, selfishness, religious extremism, and persecution. We shall now examine our identity as the persecuted people.

Discussion Questions

1. In your cultural, social, or religious context, have you encountered bigotry, religious persecution, or injustice aimed towards others? How have you, and your faith community, responded?

2. Do you sometimes fall into the trap of focusing on individual salvation more than communal/societal salvation? How might God be wanting to work in your society to bring about greater justice, righteousness, and peace? How might you and your faith community be called to partner with that work of the Spirit?

3. What is your understanding of the third person of the Trinity? Look again at the verses presented in the chart at the beginning of this chapter. Who is the Holy Spirit and what is (or should be) the Spirit's role in our lives?

4. Have there been times when you have felt that justice and love are at odds? How can we live out our calling to be both a people of love and a people of the Spirit – a people of justice? What does that look like, practically?

12

The Persecuted People

The Jerusalemite Jews expelled Jesus and sought to kill him because he healed a man who had been sick for over thirty-eight years on the Sabbath (John 5:16). After a heated theological debate, "they tried all the more to kill him; not only was he breaking the Sabbath, but he was even calling God his own Father, making himself equal with God" (5:18). Thus, there was no more religious freedom; any religious expressions that were not compatible with the Jerusalemite Jews would lead to verbal and physical violence. Consequently, Jesus could not move freely in Judea or Jerusalem, for many leaders wanted to kill him (7:1). Freedom of movement, then, was lost along with freedom of worship.

Moreover, people started gossiping about Christ, some claiming that he was a good man while others thought that he was evil, deceiving the people (7:12). Some went so far as to describe him as a demon-possessed person (7:20). When he was in Jerusalem, they wanted to capture him (7:30, 44). After a heated debate about Abraham, some sought to stone him (8:59). Also, during the Feast of Dedication, some tried to stone (10:31) and capture him (10:39). After he raised Lazarus from the dead, the Jewish leaders of Jerusalem lost all their patience and decided to kill him (11:53). They gave orders that anyone who found out where Jesus was should report it (11:57). They recognized that if his influence spread then there would be major undesired religious and political turning points. They preferred to silence him even if it involved murdering him.

The religious and political leaders persecuted Jesus as well as his followers. They decided that anyone who acknowledged that Jesus was the Messiah would be put out of the synagogue (9:22), and they expelled the man born blind who believed in Jesus (9:35). They also decided to kill Lazarus whom Jesus raised from the dead, for many believed in Jesus because of him (12:10–11). Thus, Jesus said to his disciples, "If the world hates you, keep in mind that it hated me first" (15:18). Just as the religious and political leaders persecuted Jesus, they would persecute his followers (15:20). Put differently, Christ affirmed that he was the model and example for us during seasons of persecution and said, "They will put you out of the synagogue; in fact, the time is coming when anyone who kills you will think they are offering a service to God" (16:2). The disciples would weep while the world rejoiced (16:20). John's gospel reads:

> If the world hates you, keep in mind that it hated me first. If you belonged to the world, it would love you as its own. As it is, you do not belong to the world, but I have chosen you out of the world. That is why the world hates you. Remember what I told you: "A servant is not greater than his master." If they persecuted me, they will persecute you also. If they obeyed my teaching, they will obey yours also. They will treat you this way because of my name, for they do not know the one who sent me. If I had not come and spoken to them, they would not be guilty of sin; but now they have no excuse for their sin. Whoever hates me hates my Father as well. If I had not done among them the works no one else did, they would not be guilty of sin. As it is, they have seen, and yet they have hated both me and my Father. But this is to fulfill what is written in their Law: "They hated me without reason." (15:18–25)

In light of the above passage, we need to highlight a few points. Hatred is the first step that leads to persecution. Christ repeats the word "hate" seven times. Hatred is the opposite of love, whether public or private, and consists of thoughts and feelings, and will produce evil speech and deeds. Jesus says to his relatives who did not believe in him, "The world cannot hate you, but it hates me because I testify that its works are evil" (7:7).

The world hates us because of our relationship to Jesus Christ. Jews insist on refusing the miraculous conception of Christ and his atonement. Muslims refuse his divinity, crucifixion, and resurrection. Unfortunately, these strong convictions engender hate in many places in the Middle East and some distort Christ's insistence on an inclusive love and justice. When we emphasize our Messiah, some are not only offended, but also fight back in violent ways. In short, the main sin in Israel/Palestine is hatred.

Hatred has led to wars, killing, violence, political oppression, and social persecution. In the context of such hatred, some want an Islamic state while others want a Jewish state, both employing their ideologies in order to justify marginalization and discrimination. It leads some to burn churches and spit on crosses publicly. Violence is one of the fruits of hatred. Some Jews walk the path of violence because of the history of anti-Semitism. Some Muslims walk the path of hatred because of the history of the Crusaders. In both cases, Christians are hated because they have sinned in the past, and so Christ is hated as well as his followers. Regardless of the reasons, hate is destructive and is not from God. When we hate people we act like Satan, but when we love we act like God. Unfortunately, many Christians have also walked the path of hate.

The world hates us because we are loyal to Christ. It hates us because we are not committed to the ideology of a world that refuses or marginalizes Jesus Christ. The world in John supports a false righteousness that denies God the Son, the cross, and the resurrection. The world loves its own supporters who affirm the vices of selfishness, bigotry, extremism, and violence and shun the virtues of the kingdom of God. We challenge the ideology of the world when we stand against political oppression, violations of human rights, and religious extremism. We challenge the world when we affirm forgiveness, love, peacemaking, the coexistence of Arabs and Jews, and the celebration of the existence of every Palestinian and every Jew as a gift from God. We challenge the world's ideology when we assert that God loves both Palestinians and Jews without bias and that he wants to save both peoples. They coinhabit the land and share a common existence with full equality before God.

This vision challenges Zionism and Islamism because it provides a worldview that is rooted in a common existence centered on Christ and his perception of every nation. Those who advocate such a worldview pay a high price just like the lord of justice and the king of peace who was crucified. When Christ addressed the issues of justice and righteousness, he said, "Blessed are those who are persecuted because of righteousness, for theirs is the kingdom of heaven. Blessed are you when people insult you, persecute you and falsely say all kinds of evil against you because of me. Rejoice and be glad, because great is your reward in heaven, for in the same way they persecuted the prophets who were before you" (Matt 5:10–12). The world persecutes the messengers of justice and righteousness. The word "persecute" occurs three times in the passage just quoted.

They hated Christ who came and dwelt among us, becoming human and experiencing our cultural and linguistic realities. He built bridges of communication with all the people around him. He spoke to them in wise words and forged the treasures of heaven into human metaphors that we could understand and feel. He did many good deeds that demonstrated his love, his sacrifice, and his demand that justice and righteousness should be extended, yet evil leaders hated him and still loathe his followers despite our good deeds. They hate us without good reason. Those who are far from God and threatened by Christ adopt the ideology of hatred for his followers. Whenever a person is far from God, the same person tends to be far from God's people. He or she adopts values that are not rooted in love. Instead, many adopt the vices of selfishness and hatred. Consequently, they fight against Christian values and against all those who follow Christ.

Hatred was embodied in religious and political decisions in the synagogues. Christ says, "They will put you out of the synagogue; in fact, the time is coming when anyone who kills you will think they are offering a service to God" (John 16:2). Decision makers seek to distance the followers of Christ because they don't want anyone to challenge their authority or to remind individuals, as well as communities, of their sins. These "synagogues" resist Christ with words, deeds, and oppressive policies. Hatred develops, building from an absence of love to an oppressive program of hate. It brings forth violence that deprives human beings of the most precious elements of their lives. Without doubt such killing of Christians is common in the contemporary Middle East. Christians have been killed in Iraq, Egypt, Syria, and Gaza. The extremism of Islamists, Jews, and Zionists has contributed to the promotion of hatred of Middle Eastern Christians – many have denied our right to live in dignity. As Jesus said, "In this world you will have trouble" (16:33).

How do we live in the midst of this trouble? How do we live as people who are persecuted? Persecution is something that is caused by individuals, communities, or political ideologies and entails suffering, human rights violations, and hatred. The reasons behind persecution might be political, religious, or social.

Jesus addresses religious persecution, but religion in his context entailed clear sociopolitical dimensions. The Bible mentions persecution in more than one place. Lot, for example, suffered from social persecution because he did not adopt the values of Sodom and Gomorrah (Gen 19:9). The people of his town attacked his home and his guests. We encounter the clear sociopolitical persecution of a whole nation when the Egyptians persecuted Old Testament Israel during the lifetime of Moses. They forced them to serve Egypt, enslaved them violently, issued laws of murder against the children of Old Testament Israel, and hindered the progress of their work (Exod 1:8–22). Elijah was persecuted because he did not adopt the majority religion in his country (1 Kings 19:9). Daniel was persecuted by the state because of his faith in the God of Israel and was cast into the lion's den (Dan 6:1–28). Christ also taught us that we would encounter persecution and prepared us to respond in a godly way:

I am sending you out like sheep among wolves. Therefore be as shrewd as snakes and as innocent as doves. Be on your guard; you will be handed over to the local councils and be flogged in the synagogues. On my account you will be brought before governors and kings as witnesses to them and to the Gentiles. But when they arrest you, do not worry about what to say or how to say it. At that time you will be given what to say, for it will not be you speaking, but the Spirit of your Father speaking through you. Brother will betray brother to death, and a father his child; children will rebel against their parents and have them put to death. You will be hated by everyone because of me, but the one who stands firm to the end will be saved. When you are persecuted in one place, flee to another. (Matt 10:16–23)

Jesus is asking us to be wise in addressing the dangers of persecution with prudence, and without abandoning our simplicity in Christ, and to counter hellish vices with heavenly virtues. We need to be as wise as serpents by recognizing dangers quickly and taking quick action in order to address dangerous situations. We need to be as innocent as doves: pure and wise about what is good, innocent about what is evil (Rom 16:19; Phil 2:15). Jesus guides us in order to help us shun worry and depend instead on the Holy Spirit. Furthermore, Jesus encourages us to escape from deadly dangers even if we have to leave our towns. But if we cannot escape, we persevere until the end. We should continue to hope in Christ, the victor who conquered the world, and to understand that we can hope in Christ in the midst of our tribulations. Jesus said, "In this world you will have trouble. But take heart! I have overcome the world" (John 16:33).

Perhaps it is now appropriate to write a few comments about the persecution of ISIS and similar Islamist movements that continue to appear. How can we address this kind of persecution?[1]

First, it is important to start with prayer, recognizing that God is interested in every human being in our country. The Bible says, "I urge, then, first of all, that petitions, prayers, intercession and thanksgiving be made for all people – for kings and all those in authority, that we may live peaceful and quiet lives in all godliness and holiness. This is good, and pleases God our Savior" (1 Tim 2:1–3). God must be our leader in our thoughts, and our vision, values, and convictions must be formulated in our prayer time. If we reflect on the above

---

1. Rev Dr Nabil Samara and Rev Azar Ajaj have interacted with me and given me wise counsel as I have reflected on Christian-Muslim relations in Israel.

verses, and replace the word "people" with the word "Muslims," this verse becomes clearly relevant to Christian-Muslim relations. God wants us to pray for Muslims – indeed, for all kinds of Muslims!

Second, it is important that we understand God's calling on us as individuals, churches, parachurch organizations, and communities. Within God's sovereignty we live in the midst of our beloved Muslim neighbors. According to the Bible, we understand that Christ died on the cross to redeem the world, including Muslims. The Bible says, "For God so loved the world that he gave his one and only Son, that whoever believes in him shall not perish but have eternal life" (John 3:16). Jesus commands us, "Therefore go and make disciples of all nations, baptizing them in the name of the Father and of the Son and of the Holy Spirit, and teaching them to obey everything I have commanded you. And surely I am with you always, to the very end of the age" (Matt 28:19–20). These words address the global church. In the context of the local Middle Eastern church, we can place the word "Muslims" and "Jews" in the place of the word "nations" or "world." We must pray that the Lord opens the doors for his church to obey the Great Commission in the Middle Eastern context in a missional way that empowers the local church to fulfill its divine task.

Third, we need to examine details before taking active steps. God wants us to bless our neighbors. Christ is a blessing to all the nations and in him all nations will be blessed. God said to Abraham, "All peoples on earth will be blessed through you" (Gen 12:3). We believe that this Abrahamic blessing is embodied in Christ (Eph 1:3). The Bible says, "Christ redeemed us from the curse of the law by becoming a curse for us, for it is written: 'Cursed is everyone who is hung on a pole.' He redeemed us in order that the blessing given to Abraham might come to the Gentiles through Christ Jesus, so that by faith we might receive the promise of the Spirit" (Gal 3:13–14). We are committed to being a blessing.

Nevertheless, we face some difficult challenges. In the last decade there has been a rise in Islamization and extremism among Muslims, and many sermons in mosques have rung out aggressively against Christians. Furthermore, there has been a widespread culture of anti-Christian attitudes. We need to address these challenges with accurate knowledge and count the cost wisely. Jesus said, "Suppose one of you wants to build a tower. Won't you first sit down and estimate the cost to see if you have enough money to complete it? . . . Or suppose a king is about to go to war against another king. Won't he first sit down and consider whether he is able with ten thousand men to oppose the one coming against him with twenty thousand?" (Luke 14:28–31). Nehemiah adopted this worldview when he examined the walls of Jerusalem and then recruited people for the work (Neh 3:11–18).

Fourth, we need to invest in educating ourselves to know more about Islam, its doctrines, history, sects, and cultural expectations in the Middle East. It is also important to distinguish between folk Islam and orthodox Islam, since folk Islam does not always align with the formal doctrines of Islam. We should also help Muslims to understand Christians and their faith and should present Christ in a culturally sensitive way without unnecessary linguistic or cultural barriers. Paul affirms this approach:

> To the Jews I became like a Jew, to win the Jews. To those under the law I became like one under the law . . . To those not having the law I became like one not having the law . . . so as to win those not having the law. To the weak I became weak, to win the weak. I have become all things to all people so that by all possible means I might save some. I do all this for the sake of the gospel, that I may share in its blessings. (1 Cor 9:20–23)

We can contextualize this Pauline principle by becoming like Muslims in order to win Muslims for Christ. The principle is clear even though some of the details remain cloudy. When Paul was speaking in Areopagus, he said, "For as I walked around and looked carefully at your objects of worship, I even found an altar with this inscription: to an unknown god. So you are ignorant of the very thing you worship – and this is what I am going to proclaim to you" (Acts 17:23). Put differently, it does not hurt us to read the Quran and study Islamic thought. It is desirable to understand the religion of our Muslim neighbor. Perhaps this will prove indispensable if we are to move forward as a community towards mutual respect and love.

Fifth, we need to build healthy relationships within our community. Therefore, we should invest our lives in doing good deeds and serving needy people. Jesus said, "Let your light shine before others, that they may see your good deeds and glorify your Father in heaven" (Matt 5:16). We need to be like Tabitha: "she was always doing good and helping the poor" (Acts 9:36). When she died, all the widows cried, testifying to her good deeds. They showed robes and clothes that she had made (Acts 9:36–40). The Bible warns us, "What good is it, my brothers and sisters, if someone claims to have faith but has no deeds?" (James 2:14). Such good deeds are important for building a bridge with the larger community. They embody the love of Christ in a tangible way.

Sixth, we need to respond to challenges, polemics, and violence with love, good manners, and wisdom. The Bible says, "Be wise in the way you act toward outsiders; make the most of every opportunity. Let your conversation be always full of grace, seasoned with salt, so that you may know how to answer everyone" (Col 4:5–6). Thus, we should not repay evil with evil or insult with insult; instead, we should bless those who attack us (see 1 Peter 3:9).

Seventh, we need to replace fear with love. Admittedly, there exist many dangers, polemics, and acts of violence in our context. Nevertheless, we should not be controlled by hasty reactions but by wise, godly, thoughtful actions which shape a new world rooted in love. Love reveals our true identity. The Bible says, "Whoever does not love does not know God, because God is love" (1 John 4:8). The apostle John affirms, "There is no fear in love. But perfect love drives out fear. . . . Whoever claims to love God yet hates a brother or sister is a liar. For whoever does not love their brother and sister, whom they have seen, cannot love God, whom they have not seen" (1 John 4:18–20). The logic of love is inclusive, embracing every person including all of our beloved Muslim neighbors. Loving them is the best way to drive out fear from our hearts and to clothe us with courage, as well as with the determination to extend the kingdom of Christ among our beloved Muslim neighbors.

Eighth, we should use wisely the resources that God has entrusted into our hands. These resources include human resources, different educational and medical institutions, the church, and our friends. God asked Moses, "What is that in your hand?" (Exod 4:2). It was a rod that God used to change Moses's heart and the future of God's people. Furthermore, when Andrew saw a big, hungry crowd without sufficient food, he hesitatingly said, "Here is a boy with five small barley loaves and two small fish" (John 6:9). Christ used those few resources to create a great heavenly surprise. We need to reflect on God's provisions even if they seem insignificant. God has provided our churches with physicians, lawyers, engineers, teachers, professionals, and other kinds of people. We thank the Lord that our churches – our hands – are filled with blessings that God can activate for the sake of the kingdom of Christ among Muslims.

Ninth, we need to look for partners among our Muslim brothers and sisters. There is no doubt that there are Islamists who are not willing to interact with Christians in a fair way. Nevertheless, there are moderate Muslims who are thoughtful in responding to the concerns of Christians. We can also find among Muslims people who are similar to the New Testament's Nicodemus, who was open to interacting with Christ (John 3), and Gamaliel, who stood against the persecution of the followers of Jesus. We read in the book of Acts:

> But a Pharisee named Gamaliel, a teacher of the law, who was
> honored by all the people, stood up in the Sanhedrin and ordered

that the men be put outside for a little while. Then he addressed the Sanhedrin: "Men of Israel, consider carefully what you intend to do to these men. Some time ago Theudas appeared, claiming to be somebody, and about four hundred men rallied to him. He was killed, all his followers were dispersed, and it all came to nothing. After him, Judas the Galilean appeared in the days of the census and led a band of people in revolt. He too was killed, and all his followers were scattered. Therefore, in the present case I advise you: Leave these men alone! Let them go! For if their purpose or activity is of human origin, it will fail. But if it is from God, you will not be able to stop these men; you will only find yourselves fighting against God." His speech persuaded them. (Acts 5:34–40)

Tenth, we need to recognize the role and responsibilities of political and civil authorities in keeping the social peace and upholding human rights. The Bible says, "The authorities that exist have been established by God" (Rom 13:1). Civil leaders, whether they are Jews or Muslims, are considered the servants and ministers of God. Paul writes:

For rulers are not a cause of fear for good behavior, but for evil. Do you want to have no fear of authority? Do what is good and you will have praise from the same; for it is a minister of God to you for good. But if you do what is evil, be afraid; for it does not bear the sword for nothing; for it is a minister of God, an avenger who brings wrath on the one who practices evil. Therefore it is necessary to be in subjection, not only because of wrath, but also for conscience's sake. For because of this you also pay taxes, for rulers are servants of God, devoting themselves to this very thing. (Rom 13:3–7)

Therefore, it is important not only to respect the order that God has ordained but also to wisely interact with it in ways that extend God's kingdom. We need to partner with rulers to advocate what is good and prevent what is evil.

Last but not least, it is important that Christians work together. When we are together, we are more effective and more powerful. We have all been baptized into one body regardless of our denominational background, and we have all been made to drink of one Spirit. Some of us are like an ear, others are like an eye, but we belong to the same body (1 Cor 12:12–31). We, as one body, are called to serve the one God. Our Muslim neighbors shall know our identity as Christ's disciples when we love each other (John 13:35). So let us work together and let the whole church take the whole gospel to the whole world, including our Muslim neighbors. We can work together as we empower our members and organizations at both the individual and communal level. Let us declare Christ as our personal savior and also as the savior of our culture and the whole universe. Let us be agents of reconciliation between people and God, as well as between different people. Let us prepare the way for the advent of the kingdom of Christ that overcomes persecution and transforms the season of the cross into the season of resurrection.

Now that we have discussed our identity as the people of love, the people of the Spirit, and the persecuted people, a discussion of the people of the vine as mentioned in John 15 is in order.

Discussion Questions

1. Have you – or others in your community – experienced the kind of persecution that Christ talks about in John 16? Give some examples.

2. How have you – or your community – responded to that persecution? Has that response reflected Christ's calling to love or Satan's calling to hate?

3. What is it about Jesus's testimony that leads the world to hate him and his followers? What do you think it is that the world is rejecting so adamantly and why?

4. How can we remind ourselves of who we are called to be – as people of love – in the midst of persecution?

13

The People of the Vine[1]

John 15 has encouraged many people throughout the ages. Nevertheless, it has also caused many disputes due to diverse interpretations concerning eternal security and apostasy.[2] The pertinent discussion can be found in many articles that seek to explain the denotations of the unfruitful branch in John 15:2. Interpreters claim that the unfruitful branch is (1) an apostate, (2) an unbeliever, or (3) an unfruitful believer who is under the judgment of God without losing his or her salvation. Some argue that the unfruitful branch will not be removed but lifted up. Others disagree, claiming that it will be removed completely, meaning that the believer will lose his or her salvation. Carl Laney, on the one hand, argues that the unfruitful branch is the nominal Christian, not the true believer.[3] Lewis Chafer, on the other hand, believes that the unfruitful branch is a believer who will be disciplined in this life even unto death.[4]

This theological discussion is important, but it does not relate to the Johannine context. It does not take into consideration the new world order in John. Nor does it contemplate the identity of the followers of Christ who, according to John, are the people of love, people of the Spirit, and the persecuted people. Here the evangelist adds the important detail that we are the people of the true vine.

And what is this true vine? It is Christ. Christ says, "I am the true vine, and my Father is the vinedresser" (15:1). John uses the word "true" as an adjective in several places: the true light (1:9), the true worshippers (4:23), the true bread

---

1. This section draws on an earlier work related to the seven "I am" sayings in the Gospel of John, which deals with the matter of identity from the perspective of those first-person declarations. I developed the argument and related the expression "I am the vine" to the new world order that I advocate for here. For further details, see Katanacho (كتناشو). أنا هو [I AM], 156–177.

2. Dillow, "Abiding Is Remaining," 44.

3. Laney, "Abiding Is Believing," 61.

4. Chafer, *Systematic Theology*, 7:4.

(6:32), the true vine (15:1), and the true God (17:3). All of these adjectives are related to Christ, who is the only way to the true God. John mentions the true vine to remind us of the vine that failed in fulfilling God's plan, unfaithful Israel who rejected God's commandments and now rejects Christ. On the other hand, the vine that fulfilled God's plan is embodied in and connected to Christ.

This notion does not replace Israel with the church but affirms that the dreams and hopes of Old Testament Israel are fulfilled in Christ. God is not rejecting Old Testament Israel but is fulfilling his promises in Christ. Through Christ, every believer is transformed into the New Israel. The New Testament Israel is portrayed as the branches of Christ, the true vine. Its life depends on him. As we feed on him and are nourished by him, Christ produces fruit through us so that, when the world sees our good deeds, they believe in him.

The Old Testament speaks about Israel as a vine, a metaphor found in many Old Testament texts (Ps 80:9–16; Isa 5:1–7; 27:2–5; Jer 2:21; 12:10; Ezek 15:1–8; 17:1–21; 19:10–14; Hos 10:1–2). Psalm 80 speaks of God as the vinedresser who took Israel out of Egypt and planted her in the Promised Land, desiring that the vine grow and spread in amazing ways. The glory of this vine is connected to the glory of its vinedresser. God wanted the vine to grow throughout all the earth, covering the mountains and spreading from the river to the sea. Asaph states in this psalm, "You removed a vine from Egypt; you drove out the nations and planted it. You cleared the ground before it, and it took deep root and filled the land. The mountains were covered with its shadow, and the cedars of God with its boughs. It was sending out its branches to the sea and its shoots to the River" (Ps 80:8–11).

Isaiah informs us that the vinedresser did everything possible to produce a fruitful vine, but the vine produced bad grapes, ignoring justice and righteousness (Isa 5:1–7). Isaiah helps us to understand that the problem with the vine is not the vinedresser but the corruption of the people. He says, "For the vineyard of the Lord of hosts is the house of Israel and the men of Judah his delightful plant. Thus he looked for justice, but behold, bloodshed; for righteousness, but behold, a cry of distress" (Isa 5:7).

How can this vine escape the just divine judgment? How can it be saved? How can it fulfill the vision of the vinedresser? Asaph explains that the answer to these questions can be found when we reflect on the relationship of the vine to its vinedresser. God has chosen the vine to be his son (Ps 80:14–15). Indeed, the vine is a *chosen* son. The hope of the vine is connected to this relationship and to the person that represents it. This person is the leader, the man of God, the right-hand man, and the chosen Adam. He is the son of Adam and the Son of Man who sits at the right hand of God, the Son of Man who sits at the right hand of power (Matt 26:64). He is also our protector against apostasy and our means for abiding in God and receiving eternal life. In short, Christ is the true vine.

Christ is the vine that grants life to its branches; he is the source of our fruit. He is the one who unites us, for the vine gathers all the branches into one tree. These branches – different in size and color – produce different amounts of fruit. The branches may be African, Asian, European, American, or Australian, and are young, old, light and dark. Yet all of them are connected to one vine. Only through the vine are these branches truly united and living. In the vine there are three kinds of branches: fruitless, fruitful, and even more fruitful (15:2). Let us look more closely at these branches.

It is obvious that the life of the branches depends on the vine. Christ said, "apart from me you can do nothing" (15:5). Christ is Christianity's strength, power, and life. Thus, our worship and life must focus on him. We, in the Middle East, live in the midst of ecclesiastical diversity. We know Catholic, Orthodox, Oriental Orthodox, Protestant, and Messianic Jewish congregations. It seems that the vine in Israel/Palestine has five main branches which vary in their fruitfulness, even though they belong to the same vine. The church was divided at Chalcedon in AD 451 when some refused the decisions of the council that bears that city's name. Consequently, the non-Chalcedonian churches were formed. Today, the churches known as Oriental Orthodox include Coptic, Armenian Orthodox, Syrian Orthodox, and Ethiopian Orthodox.

Other churches divided in the eleventh century and thus the identities of the Catholic and Orthodox churches were established. The Catholic Church was divided in the sixteenth century and the Protestant churches were born. Almost every five hundred years the world witnessed a major church division. In the twentieth century, however, several churches worked hard to join in fellowship and to express a visible unity. Many churches recognized each other as valid branches belonging to the same vine. Middle Eastern Christians understood that either we stick together or disappear. Therefore, we should celebrate the diversity of our brothers and sisters instead of fighting each other. We recognize that God is the final and highest judge who has allowed us to be part of the same vine.

Christ asks us to abide in him. When we center our lives on Christ and obey his commandments, we shall be fruitful and fulfill God's call for his church. The fruit of the vine is peace, love, and joy. Christ said, "Peace I leave with you; my peace I give you" (14:27). He said, "As the Father has loved me, so have I loved you. Now remain in my love" (15:9). Also, he said, "I have told you this so that my joy may be in you and that your joy may be complete" (15:11).

It is clear that the peace, love, and joy of Christ are intended for us and that we shall experience these christological virtues and conquer the evils of the world. This fruit is connected to the identity of Christ as the vine and to his teachings, so we must abide in Jesus Christ, the incarnated God, who fulfills all the longings of the Old Testament. He has shown us the true meaning of truth, freedom, peace, love, and integrity, and has offered us the virtues of the kingdom of God. When we contemplate the incarnated Logos and the written word, and abide in the vine prayerfully, we will bring forth abundant fruit. Christ said, "If you remain in me and my words remain in you, ask whatever you wish, and it will be done for you" (15:7).

There is no doubt that abiding in Christ is essential. But in what kind of Christ do we abide? Who is this Christ in whom we believe? Christianity has focused throughout the ages on the identity of Christ, affirming that he is fully God and fully human and studying the details that relate to his identity. These are true affirmations and an important task, yet in Israel/Palestine we need to reflect on Christ as the vine that connects separate branches together. We need to know the vine that does not only bring forth personal salvation but also brings forth the salvation of the whole community. How can Christ be the vine of Palestine and of Israel?

Christ is not only the savior of individuals. He is also the savior of the Palestinian and Israeli communities. Therefore, we ask how Christ can empower us to create a culture of forgiveness and a community of forgivers.[5] How can we build a culture of love and mutual acceptance that refuses to hate? There is no doubt that the salvation offered by Christ is more than personal salvation that offers heaven to our spirits. Rather, it is the kind of salvation that brings the kingdom of heaven down to earth and establishes justice and peace. Christ has saved us through the cross, but we taste the fruit of his salvation through his fruitful branches. We are the messengers of the vine to a world that lacks peace, love, and joy. We must talk about unity because we are the people of unity. This is the topic of the next chapter; it is very visible in the prayer of Jesus in John 17.

---

5. I owe this expression to Rula Mansour who teaches at Nazareth Evangelical College in Israel.

Discussion Questions

1. What significant "branches" – or church divisions – exist in your own context? How important are those divisions perceived to be? Are the divisions within the church bringing forth fruit or standing in the way of fruit?

2. Reflect on your experiences of church diversity. Do you find it difficult to love and appreciate your brothers and sisters from other church backgrounds? What has communion with other believers taught you (or what *might* it teach you) about God, about Christ, and about unity?

3. Read John 15:1–17. What is the connection that Jesus draws between being people of the vine and people of love?

4. Read Galatians 5:22–23. To what degree are you experiencing the fruit of the Spirit – the fruit born of abiding in the vine – in your own life? What steps might you take to bear more fruit?

14

The People of Unity

Unity is a prominent theme in the prayer of Jesus in John 17. The Gospel of John highlights the issue of prayer in the farewell discourses (13:31–17:26). In addition to the long prayer in chapter 17, we encounter seven statements that testify to the importance of prayer.

1	And I will do whatever you ask in my name, so that the Father may be glorified in the Son (14:13).
2	You may ask me for anything in my name, and I will do it (14:14).
3	If you remain in me and my words remain in you, ask whatever you wish, and it will be done for you (15:7).
4	You did not choose me, but I chose you and appointed you so that you might go and bear fruit – fruit that will last – and so that whatever you ask in my name the Father will give you (15:16).
5	In that day you will no longer ask me anything. Very truly I tell you, my Father will give you whatever you ask in my name (16:23).
6	Until now you have not asked for anything in my name. Ask and you will receive, and your joy will be complete (16:24).
7	In that day you will ask in my name. I am not saying that I will ask the Father on your behalf (16:26).

It is clear that here is a turning point in the prayer life of the disciples: a new age is dawning in which the disciples will pray to the Father in the name of Jesus.

Jews in the first century were a people of prayer. They prayed in the temple, in synagogues and in their homes. The temple was called a house of prayer (Isa 56:7). They offered prayers and sacrifices twice a day in the temple, at the third and ninth hour of the day. They counted the hours according to the rising of the sun, following the first-century Roman custom which limited a day to twelve hours (see John 11:9).[1] The KJV Bible says, "Now Peter and John went up together into the temple at the hour of prayer, being the ninth hour" (Acts 3:1). Three in the afternoon is the ninth hour. Furthermore, Jews prayed in the synagogues on Saturdays and feast days. Usually, a person stood up to pray in an audible voice and then all the worshippers said "amen."

Roman Time	Modern Time
The third hour after sunrise	3 sunny hours + 6 dark hours after midnight = 9 hours or 9 a.m.
The ninth hour after sunrise	9 sunny hours + 6 dark hours after midnight = 15 hours or 3 p.m.

Some scholars suggest that first-century Jewish prayers included the following: the prayer "Hear O Israel" (Deut 6:4) at sunrise; the 9 a.m. prayer at the temple; the 3 p.m. prayer at the temple; and the prayer "Hear O Israel" at sunset.[2] Worshippers at Qumran prayed without offering temple sacrifices, affirming the importance of pure hearts in worship.[3] The Jews also prayed at home at meal times. They were obedient to the text in Deuteronomy 8:10 which states, "When you have eaten and are satisfied, praise the Lord your God for the good land he has given you."

Put differently, Jesus of Nazareth did not invent prayer. Yet he directed it and shaped it in a unique way. Prayer was now associated with abiding in him, was related to his name, was connected to joy and fruit, and was associated with glorifying the Father as well as the Son. Prayer is now part of our relationship with Christ and participation in his mission. It is missional by definition, as well as christological. The best theology of prayer is christological and missional, focused on Christ and his mission. The best Christology is rooted in a Trinitarian theology. We shall unpack these claims as we study the prayer of chapter 17. We need to understand the concept of unity in the context of relating to Christ, his mission, prayer, and holy longings. In short, longing for unity, fervent prayers, and holy desires that honor Christ are essential for bringing about unity.

---

1. The Bible uses the Roman system more than once. For example, we encounter their timing system in the parable of the workers of the vine. In this parable, the workers were expected to work up to 12 hours (see Matt 20:9–20).

2. See Easley, "Prayer Customs."

3. Easley, 49.

Christ offers his prayer to the Father in six parts, repeating the expression "Father" at the beginning of each part (17:1, 5, 11, 21, 24, and 25).[4] He prays for himself (17:1–5), for the disciples (17:6–19), and for those who will believe through the disciples (17:20–26). Since his prayer is part of the farewell discourses before he goes to the cross, he places within it the most important things on his mind at that time. Let us look more closely at this amazing prayer.

First, the first five verses affirm the glorification of the Son both at the beginning and end of the passage (vv. 1, 5). We know that the Son was glorified before the incarnation/enhumanization (17:5). We have seen his glory in the incarnation (1:14), and we have seen some of his glory in the signs during his earthly ministry (2:11; 11:4). However, his glory was not perceived during his life in a fallen world. The glories and effectiveness of the signs were limited and temporal. John's Gospel explains, "Even after Jesus had performed so many signs in their presence, they still would not believe in him" (12:37). But the glory that he is praying for in John 17:5 is associated with his death and resurrection. At the end of his public ministry, Jesus prayed, saying, "'Father, glorify your name!' Then a voice came from heaven, 'I have glorified it, and will glorify it again'" (12:28). The Son glorified the Father throughout his life and ministry, and now he would glorify him through his death and resurrection.

When Judas surrendered to the path of murder, he left the Last Supper to betray Jesus. Then Jesus said, "Now the Son of Man is glorified and God is glorified in him" (13:31). The context confirms that Christ is referencing his death. Perhaps it is important to highlight that the glory of the resurrection is visible, unlike the glory of the Son before the incarnation. The glory of the resurrection is permanent, unlike the glory of the signs. After the resurrection, Christ ascended to heaven and sat down at the right side of the Father. Then the Holy Spirit was poured out. The Fourth Gospel makes a startling claim: "Up to that time the Spirit had not been given, since Jesus had not yet been glorified" (7:37). The Holy Spirit shall glorify the Son (16:14) until his second coming. John 17:1–5 affirms the interconnection between glory and the gift of the Father. We encounter the term "give," or a related word, in verses 2 and 4.[5] The Father gave the Son authority to grant eternal life (v. 2); he gave him work to finish (v. 4); he gave him people who believed in him (vv. 6, 9, 12, 24); he gave him words (v. 8); he also gave him the glory that would lead to the unity of the people of Christ (vv. 22, 24). Thus, the glory is connected to

---

4. See Malatesta, "Literary Structure."

5. The word "give" or a related form occurs seventeen times in chapter 17: in verse 2 (three times), 4, 6 (twice), 7, 8 (twice), 9, 11, 12, 14, 22 (twice), and 24 (twice).

unity and to the divine gift – that is, receiving eternal life, knowing God and his messenger, Jesus Christ (v. 3). This knowledge is related to the mission of Christ. Christ is a messenger and his mission continues through his disciples. Their unity influences their mission and consequently marks the mission of Christ as well as the perceived glory of the triune God.

There is no doubt that the issue of unity among people is connected to the unity of the Father and the Son. When Christ prayed, he said, "I have given them the glory that you gave me, that they may be one as we are one" (17:22). The unity of the Father and the Son appears explicitly in several places in chapter 17. The following table demonstrates the interconnectedness between the unity of the Father and the Son and the unity of the people of Christ.

They were yours; you gave them to me (v. 6).
Now they know that everything you have given me comes from you (v. 7).
All I have is yours, and all you have is mine. And glory has come to me through them (v. 10).
That they may be one as we are one (v. 11).
That all of them may be one, Father, just as you are in me and I am in you (v. 21).
That they may be one as we are one (v. 22).
I in them and you in me – so that they may be brought to complete unity (v. 23).

The unity of the Trinity, especially the unity of the Father and the Son, is essential for the unity of the followers of Christ. So, we must ask: What is the nature of unity between the first and second persons of the Trinity? The unity of the Trinity in the Eastern tradition depends on the eternal love of the Father. The Father is the first cause of this love, and his granting of himself completely caused the birth of the Son and the procession of the Holy Spirit.

This reality is not connected to time or space or to a worldview rooted in creation. There was no time before or after the birth of the Son or the procession of the Holy Spirit. Time is irrelevant. In other words, the birth of the Son and the procession of the Spirit are not connected to the economic Trinity but to the ontological Trinity. All the persons of the Trinity are eternal and have no beginning. At the same time, they relate to each other in unique ways.

The Son and the Holy Spirit have the same essence as the Father. The Son is fully God born of the Father who is fully God. He is born not created and has the same essence as the Father. The Holy Spirit is fully God. He proceeds from the Father and is not created. He, too, has the same essence as the Father. The second and third persons of the Trinity love the Father as the Father loves them. The Son expresses his love by complete obedience to the Father. Thus, the

Father – through his love and the giving of himself completely in the eternal generation of the Son and procession of the Holy Spirit – is the first cause for the unity of the Trinity.[6] The love of the Father is like the foundation of unity for the Trinity.[7]

Our own unity with this love is the climax of embodying the divine commission, which is related to how Christians interact with the world. The term "world" occurs eighteen times in John 17.[8] The denotation of the word depends on the context. It might mean creation, all human beings, or those who refused Christ. Put differently, the prayer of Jesus in chapter 17 provokes a question related to the nature of the relationship of the believer to the world: should the believer be against the world?

If so, the believer determines that the world is evil, and consequently, there are no agreements between church and society. Churches must be separate from the world because the world is evil. Churches must focus on saving souls and on heaven. They must be patient until this bad season is over. This world is passing away and our true home is heaven. The world is rooted in evil and thus we must shun it and even fight against it. The church is like the ark of Noah and the world is drowning. We have to call all those who believe to enter the ark of salvation.

Alternatively, the believer might be in concord with the world. In that case, the believer becomes like salt that is mixed with dirt and thus loses its saltiness. Or perhaps believers believe themselves to be greater than the world and consequently feel superior, full of pride, and proud of their moral superiority. They become like the Pharisees, and the world in their eyes is like the immoral tax collectors.

Perhaps there is another way to interact with the world, though. The table below summarizes the data so far:

The believer is against the world	The believer is greater than the world	The believer is in concord with the world	The believer is sent to the world
→ ←	↓ ↑	⬅➡	⬇ ←

---

6. Scouteris, "People of God," 406.

7. In Western traditions, the unity of the Trinity is related to the one essence of the Father, Son, and Holy Spirit.

8. We observe this in verses 5, 6, 9, 11 (twice), 12, 13, 14 (twice), 15, 16 (twice), 18 (twice), 21, 23, 24, and 25.

When the believer is sent to the world . . .	. . . the outcome shall be that the world is directed towards God
⬇⬅	↻

Jesus offers us three prepositions that help us to understand the relationship of the believer to the world. These little words are "of," "in," and "to." Jesus says that his disciples are in the world, but they are not of the world – he sends them to the world.

1. Christ's disciples are not of the world because they refuse to adopt its values, moral standards, behavioral patterns, and its understanding of God, his creation, the future, and salvation. They are part of the human race, but they live among that race with divine convictions.

2. Although Christians are not from this world, they are still in the world. We are part of the society and the state in which we live. We are part of our country whether we are Israelis or Palestinians.

3. God sent believers to the world to extend his kingdom.

We need to maintain the equilibrium between the three pertinent prepositions. Otherwise, we will lose our identity, purpose, and meaning in life.

In	Of	To
We are in the world	We are not of the world	We are sent to the world

Our mission depends on our collective identity. When we are united by our love, then the world will believe that the Father has sent the Son (17:21) and discover the love of the Father. In light of this reality, we wonder about the Christian-Christian relationships in Palestine and Israel. Do we consider other denominations as heretics or as part of our Christian family? Is Christ our way towards unity or towards division? Adopting a denominational, narrow-minded perspective leads us to judge others and condemn them as heretics or as false teachers. We wonder, therefore, how we can define the identity of Christians and discern who is a Christian and who is not. What are our responsibilities towards those who belong to other Christian denominations? Let us address the first question followed by the second.

Christians in Israel/Palestine don't agree on a definition of who is a Christian. Some say a Christian is a person who has been baptized as a baby in a specific denomination and is faithful to the teachings of that denomination.

Members of this group may claim that those in other denominations are not truly Christian but rather heretics and false teachers. A second group of Christians argues that true Christians are those who have heard the gospel and accepted it. A third group claims that a Christian is one who has accepted a specific list of doctrines such as the Nicene Creed. In addition, several groups claim that Christianity is exclusive to their own group. Some might argue that they represent pure Christianity while others are impure. Denominations struggle as each denies the legitimacy of the other, viewing the other through a lens of suspicion. Claiming that the other is a heretic, the response might be, "We are the true believers." Trust is lost and there are no bridges of communication between the polarized groups. Thus, we ask: Who is a Christian?

The Bible uses the term "Christian" three times (Acts 11:26; 26:28; 1 Pet 4:16): the disciples of Jesus were called "Christians" for the first time in Antioch (Acts 11:26); King Agrippa used the word when he asked Paul, "Do you think that in such a short time you can persuade me to be a Christian?" (Acts 26:28); and "Christian" is also used in Peter's first epistle, as the apostle addresses the issue of persecution against the followers of Jesus (1 Pet 4:16).

The Bible uses the expression "born of God" to define what is required to be a Christian. Let us look more closely at some biblical texts in the first epistle of John to discover the requirements that define the one who is born of God:

1. "Everyone who believes that Jesus is the Christ is born of God" (1 John 5:1).

2. "No one who is born of God will continue to sin" (1 John 3:9; cf. 1 John 5:18).

3. "For everyone born of God overcomes the world" (1 John 5:4).

4. "If you know that he is righteous, you know that everyone who does what is right has been born of him" (1 John 2:29).

5. "Dear friends, let us love one another, for love comes from God. Everyone who loves has been born of God and knows God" (1 John 4:7).

These texts define the identity of a Christian, giving a definition that is not rooted in a denominational framework but is instead inseparable from specific characteristics in the life of the one born of God. These characteristics include faith in Jesus Christ, his incarnation, death, resurrection, and identity. Moreover, the one born of God does not continue to sin but lives in righteousness and justice. The life of such a person is full of the love of God and love for people, especially those in his or her proximity.

Love, faith, righteousness, and justice are virtues that cannot be absent from, or insignificant in, the person born of God. Christians must be people of love, faith, righteousness, and justice. Our Christian praxis should distance itself from denominational exclusivism, claims of moral or spiritual superiority, and competitions related to historical preeminence. Instead, our prominence must be seen in the love, faith, righteousness, and justice that we extend to all people, especially our brothers and sisters in faith. Let us follow Jesus as people who are born of God – as the body of Christ – not within a denominational worldview that amputates parts of the body in the name of denominational purity. All Christians who are born of God are my brothers and my sisters, regardless of their denominational background. How, then, can we express this unity in practical ways?

Although, as Christians, we don't have doctrinal or institutional unity, we must commit ourselves to the unity of Christian love. Beginning by loving Christians of other denominations and serving them wholeheartedly as our brothers and sisters in faith, we must invest time and effort to reach out to all the members of our Christian faith. Furthermore, we need to look for and encourage organizations or frameworks that bring us together, such as the World Council of Churches and other organizations with similar goals.

It is not enough to meet with other Christians, though. Praying for all members of the body of the Messiah is important, as well as seeking to bless them by word and deed and supporting their ministries whenever possible. Working together to build bridges of communication and respect is also essential. This does not mean that we are abandoning our unique convictions, but our Christian convictions must always be rooted in such love, and we should celebrate interdenominational marriage as long as the couple is committed to following Jesus and living a life of love, faith, righteousness, and justice. We can also encourage common worship and wash each other's feet in love and without hypocrisy. This unity has missional implications. It points the world to Jesus, the head of the one church which obeys the one Lord. Having argued that we should be the people of unity, it is important, now, to unpack the centrality of the cross in shaping our identity and to argue that we are also the people of the cross.

Discussion Questions

1. Prayer was a significant aspect of religious life in first-century Judaism. In your own cultural and religious context, what is the role of prayer, both personal and communal?

2. In your social context, what does it mean to be a person who is *in* the world, and sent *to* the world, but is not *of* the world? What are some of the specific challenges to holding this balance?

3. What role does prayer have in your life? Do you see it as being an essential part of unity – between you and God and you and the church?

4. How would you define what it means to be a Christian? Revisiting the list of passages from 1 John, does your definition line up with John's definition? Is there anything that needs to be added or subtracted from your definition?

5. John seems to indicate that one cannot be a Christian without being a member of the people of love. Since this is a theme that recurs over and over in John's Gospel and his first epistle, what is the connection between being a person of love and a person of unity? How might you take concrete steps towards love and unity in your own community?

15

The People of the Cross

We propose the following sequence of events as we look at the last week in the life of Jesus. On Saturday, Jesus raised Lazarus from the dead before entering Jerusalem on Palm Sunday. Monday, he cleansed the temple. Tuesday, he challenged the religious leaders. Wednesday, he wept over Jerusalem. On Thursday, he washed the feet of the disciples and ate the last supper with them.

After the meal, Christ prayed in Gethsemane before he was arrested. Here, the sequence of events might be as follows: arrest, tribunal before Ananias, tribunal before Caiaphas, imprisonment, tribunal before all the leaders of the Sanhedrin, tribunal before Pilate, then a tribunal before Herod Antipas, and a second tribunal before Pilate. Then Roman soldiers mocked Jesus, flogged him, put a crown of thorns on his head, and forced him to carry his cross along the Via Dolorosa before his crucifixion, death, and burial.

The following table is a clarification of some of the most significant events in the last hours of Jesus's life. It is not intended to be an accurate timetable of events, as we are not given all the details, but rather an aid to imagine what it might have been like. The table delineates events after Jesus washed the feet of the disciples, prayed in Gethsemane, and was arrested.

The Proposed Time	The Event
12:00–1:00 a.m.	The arrest of Jesus on Friday after midnight
1:00–1:30 a.m.	Tribunal before Ananias
1:30–2:30 a.m.	Tribunal before Caiaphas
2:30–4:00 a.m.	Imprisonment
4:00–5:00 a.m.	Tribunal before the leaders of the Sanhedrin
5:00–5:30 a.m.	Tribunal before Pilate
5:30–6:30 a.m.	Tribunal before Herod Antipas
6:30–7:00 a.m.	Second tribunal before Pilate and issuing the decision of execution

7:00–7:30 a.m.	The Roman soldiers mocked Christ, flogged him, and put the crown of thorns on his head
7:30–9:00 a.m.	Carrying the cross on the Via Dolorosa
9:00–12:00 p.m.	Jesus hung on the cross during daylight
12:00–3:00 p.m.	Jesus hung on the cross and the sun disappeared completely
3:00 p.m.	He gave up his spirit into the hands of the Father
3:30–5:00 p.m.	He was buried
Sunday early morning	After Saturday, and while it was dark on Sunday morning, Christ rose from the dead

We shall now explain the details of the arrest, tribunals, and crucifixion as depicted by John. After his farewell discourses (John 13:31–17:26), Jesus walked with his disciples to the Kidron valley (18:1) and entered a garden which he used to visit with his disciples, the garden of Gethsemane (Matt 26:36; Mark 14:32), which means the garden of the oil press. Judas, the traitor, approached them with a band of Roman soldiers and officers of the chief priests. The soldiers were Roman soldiers while the officers were Jewish guards who served in temple security. The Greek word (*Speiran*; σπεῖραν) in John 18:3 is equivalent to the word "band." It literally means a thousand soldiers. Usually, a Roman band included 240 horsemen and 760 marching soldiers, with a commander or captain who was called, literally, "a leader of a thousand" (χιλίαρχος; John 18:12). But the linguistic evidence is not conclusive, for the word can also refer to a group of soldiers that is less than a thousand.[1] Some, therefore, suggest that the number of soldiers was around two hundred.[2] In any case, Jesus was arrested and was taken first to Ananias, who was the high priest during the years 15–6 BC. Five of his children became high priests after him, and his son in law, Caiaphas, was the high priest during the time of the crucifixion of Christ.[3] Caiaphas, who was the high priest during the years AD 18–38, wanted to get rid of Jesus and suggested killing him (John 11:49–50). He also opposed the followers of Jesus and was involved in the arrest of Peter and John (see Acts 4:5–6).

Jesus was taken to Ananias first and then to Caiaphas, who asked Jesus about his disciples and his teaching in order to discover the extent of his military and political power and sharpen the accusations. Thus, the Jewish

1. Carson, *Gospel According to John*, 577.

2. Beasley-Murray, *John*, 322.

3. Carson, *Gospel According to John*, 580–581.

authorities broke the law by holding a tribunal during the night. The high priests were seeking false testimony against Jesus (Matt 26:59) and when the testimonies differed, they did not question the veracity of the witnesses. Legal protocol required that accusations were to be proved. Legal proceedings began by listening to the defenders of the accused person, the accused was not interrogated, and it was illegal for witnesses to accuse the arrested person. Furthermore, it was illegal to hit the accused person before condemning him.

Jesus challenged these legal violations and this oppression. When Jesus was slapped by a temple guard, he did not accept the offense, but challenged the oppression with truth. He rightly resisted with logic by raising appropriate questions: "Why do you ask me? . . . Why do you slap me?" (John 18:20, 23). He also resisted oppression by raising pertinent issues in the context of his public ministry. He said, "I have spoken openly to the world. . . . I always taught in synagogues or at the temple, where all the Jews come together. I said nothing in secret. Why question me? Ask those who heard me" (18:20–21). In this way, Jesus turned the other cheek, for he sought to interact with his oppressors from the logic of love, truth, and justice, resisting oppression with good. After his tribunal before Caiaphas, he was judged by all the high priests and elders (Matt 27:1).

In the morning, Jesus was brought before Pilate, the Roman governor who ruled Judea during the years AD 26–36. He was a violent dictator. Luke informs us that Pilate killed many Galileans, mixing their blood with their sacrifices (Luke 13:1). The historian Josephus informs us that Pilate massacred a large number of Samaritans.[4] Several Jews conspired against Jesus, seeking to spill his blood at the hands of Pilate. Wanting him to perceive Jesus as a political threat and a threat to Rome, they said, "We have found this man subverting our nation. He opposes payment of taxes to Caesar and claims to be Messiah, a king . . . he stirs up the people all over Judea by his teaching" (Luke 23:2, 5). Thus, the dictator confronted the righteous one; the governor oppressed the Christ. Judicial justice failed; it was blind. Instead of vindicating the oppressed, it spread evil. The governor, Pilate, ceased being an agent of justice because he was consumed with pleasing those who could help him stay in power.

Pilate ordered the scourging of Christ before issuing the order for his crucifixion, but both Matthew and Mark (Matt 27:26; Mark 5:15) speak of the scourging of Christ after the decision to crucify him. Carson explains that there were three kinds of scourging: (1) the first was *Fustigatio*. The least severe, it didn't pose a threat to life and was for lesser crimes. (2) The second

---

4. Josephus, *Antiquities of the Jews*, 18.4.1–2.

was *Flagellatio*. Harsher than the first, it was reserved for crimes that were dangerous and serious. (3) The third was *Verberatio*. Connected to crucifixion, the floggers continued to whip the person until they were tired or the person died. The whips had leather strips with hooked bones or metal at their edges that ripped the flesh, causing much bleeding and damage. The guilty person usually died from loss of blood.[5] Perhaps Christ was whipped twice, once before the execution order was issued – as we read in John 19:1 – and then before the crucifixion.

After Jesus's first encounter with Pilate, and his first whipping, he was taken to Herod Antipas. Herod despised Jesus, and his soldiers mocked the Holy One of Israel. They dressed him in an elegant robe and returned him to Pilate (Luke 23:11). Pilate wanted to release him, but he released Barabbas instead. Pilate affirmed three times that he could not find anything wrong in Jesus (John 18:38; 19:4, 6). Nevertheless, he gave the order to crucify him (John 19:16). Accused of being a king, Jesus was sarcastically described as a king by Pilate (John 18:39; 19:14–15, 19, 21) and consequently walked the *Via Dolorosa*. After being whipped and crowned with thorns, he carried a beam of wood that was part of his cross, the crossbar, and headed to the place of crucifixion.

Before the condemned criminal was crucified, the soldiers unclothed him, tied his hands and whipped his back and legs with bone lashes or metal hooks. Consequently, the condemned bled, and the loss of blood made it difficult for him to live more than a few hours. Afterwards, he carried a heavy beam of wood. The weight of the whole cross might be 100 kg and the horizontal beam might weigh between 35 and 50 kg. The condemned wore a sign around his neck explaining his guilt, and the same sign was nailed to the cross. Jesus's sign read, "Jesus of Nazareth King of the Jews." Once they reached the place of crucifixion outside the city walls, the soldiers offered the condemned some wine mixed with myrrh to numb the pain, but Christ refused to drink it (Mark 15:23). The condemned was laid on the ground over the horizontal beam and his hands were nailed to it. Then he was hung on the vertical beam and his feet were nailed with a long nail of about 15 cm. On the cross there was also a small piece of wood that allowed the crucified to sit, but this lengthened his life and, consequently, his suffering. The person on the cross was not able to breathe, so to take a breath, he would lift himself, but every time he did, his pierced hands and feet caused more pain. When the soldiers wanted to expedite death, they usually broke the person's legs. With broken legs the crucified could not lift his body to take a breath and thus suffocated and died. A crucified person might

---

5. Carson, *Gospel According to John*, 597.

also die due to carnivorous birds that gathered to feed on the bodies. Jesus hung on the cross for six hours (Mark 15:25, 34), from 9 a.m. until 3 p.m. During these six hours, the sun disappeared for three hours from noon until 3 p.m.

The cross was the cruelest means of execution, causing an enormous amount of pain. The Romans believed that it was worse than being beheaded, being burned to death, or being fed to lions. One philosopher wrote about it as follows:

> Can anyone be found who would prefer wasting away in pain dying limb by limb, or letting out his life drop by drop, rather than expiring once for all? Can any man by found willing to be fastened to the accursed tree, long sickly, already deformed, swelling with ugly wounds on shoulders and chest, and drawing the breath of life amid long drawn-out agony? He would have many excuses for dying even before mounting the cross.[6]

Palestinian poets have also been impacted by the cross. They have endured many wars, displacements, and brutal oppression. Consequently, they have seen the cross as an embodiment of their struggles against evil.[7] These poets do not speak about the crucified Christ because they are Christians but because of sociopolitical similarities between the first and the twentieth centuries in Palestine. In fact, some of these poets are Muslims. Mitri Raheb explains the contribution of Palestinian poets, especially Mahmoud Darwish, who saw the cross of Christ as an embodiment of Palestinian suffering and the resistance of evil.[8] Raheb sees the geopolitical and social Palestinian realities as the best hermeneutical lens for understanding God.[9] He uses this hermeneutical approach to address the cross and affirms that the cross is the best way to describe the Palestinian identity.[10] He states that Palestine and its people have been distinguished by the mark of suffering throughout history, and consequently, they have become the people of the cross.[11] Thus Palestine is a crucified land, and its people are crucified for they have been oppressed by several empires. The cross became a symbol for the Palestinian prisoner and for the martyr who sacrificed his or her life for the sake of spreading truth or

6. Hengel, *Crucifixion*, 31.

7. Abu Shawar (أبو شاور). تطوّر الإتجاه الوطنيّ [The evolution of the national trend], 36–41.

8. Raheb and Henderson, *Cross in Contexts*, loc. 1460 of 2340.

9. Raheb, *Faith in the Face of Empire*.

10. Raheb and Henderson, *Cross in Contexts*, loc. 337 of 2340.

11. Raheb and Henderson, loc. 2288 of 2340.

for resisting an oppressive empire.[12] Similar to Christ, Palestinians have become victims of state terrorism and religious terrorism.[13]

Raheb may have overstated the importance of the sociopolitical dimension of the cross, but he is right in affirming it. He has also exaggerated the geopolitical and social continuities between Christ and Palestinians throughout history, and he has therefore overlooked the importance of faithful adherence to the divine covenant in non-Palestinian geographical areas in both Old and New Testaments. It is important to remember God's activities in Egypt, Iraq, Iran, and the diaspora. It is equally important to observe that God has worked not only with the poor but also with kings and different layers of society. God has been active outside Palestine and in many nations, including among the rich and the poor.

Furthermore, it is important to observe the many other aspects of the cross which are as important as the sociopolitical aspects, if not more so. John Stott and Fleming Rutledge, for example, emphasize the role of the cross in saving sinners. On the cross, the Father offered his Son as a substitutionary atonement. They highlight the holiness of God, the sin of human beings, and redemption, justification, and reconciliation.[14]

Moltmann explains the impact of the cross on our understanding of the identity of God – that is, the crucified God.[15] The Father suffered when he sacrificed his only begotten Son, and the Son suffered as he fully obeyed the Father.[16] In this way, the cross is not only about redemption, it is also about the nature of God. In the cross we encounter the crucified God who suffers. The Father suffered by offering his Son and by seeing him humiliated and cursed on a cross. The Son suffered from political and socioreligious oppression, and he suffered because of the sin of human beings. In other words, he experienced the suffering of body and soul and carried the sins of humanity. When the Father hid his face, the Son's pain intensified and so he cried out: "My God, My God, why have you forsaken me?" On the cross God also suffered with those who suffer. He experienced abandonment, shame and betrayal. Also, he joined the community of crucified criminals, and we can even say that he was considered a terrorist. The Greek word translated as "robber" was actually used to denote terrorists who opposed the Roman Empire.

12. Raheb and Henderson, loc. 1247 of 2340.
13. Raheb and Henderson, loc. 730 of 2340.
14. Stott, *Cross of Christ*; Rutledge, *Crucifixion*.
15. Moltmann, *Crucified God*, Kindle Edition.
16. Moltmann, *Crucified God*, loc. 4272 of 8106.

In short, we can reflect on the cross historically, salvifically, politically, and sociologically.[17] Like Moltmann, we can consider it theologically and reflect on the nature of the crucified God. In addition, the cross is not only something we look at but also something we look through. That is, it is not only a piece of wood but also a lens through which we see the whole world. It is not only a historical event but also a celestial saving reality. The cross is a way of living and the mark of discipleship. We die as we obey God; we die for the sake of affirming our love for our enemies.

We Palestinians in Israel are reminded that it was forbidden to crucify first-class citizens in the Roman Empire. As using the insult of the cross against Roman citizens was banned, only second-class citizens were crucified. Jesus was a second-class citizen in the kingdom of Rome but a first-class citizen in the kingdom of God. Jesus embodied a life that carries the cross every day – as the cross entails resisting evil, denying self, and obeying God. The cross is the path for resisting sociopolitical discrimination against Arabs (and some Jews) in Israel. From the perspective of the cross, all people are equal; all people are convicted sinners and lack righteousness. But the cross saves us from the false peace offered by oppressive states and corrupt religious authorities. The peace of the cross does not depend on silencing the voice of truth by violence but on exposing sociopolitical violence through an insistence on love for the enemy, forgiveness, truth, justice, equality, and reconciliation with God and neighbor. This is the mindset of the cross that reflects divine standards. The cross is the path through which we are saved from the violence advocated by Caiaphas and Pilate.

The cross saves us from an ethnic Jewish state, paving the way for a kingdom of equality in which membership is for those who carry the cross and are willing to be crucified for the sake of God and his kingdom. In the cross we encounter the loud drums of political terrorism wielded against the soft voice of love, justice, and mercy. In the cross we reflect on empires' oppression of marginalized groups. In the cross we find the power to forgive, the kingdom of love, and the determination to fight all forms of evil with good. The cross embodies a loud paradox: in our weakness we become strong and in our death life spreads. We are the people of the cross in a country that has many crucifiers. But those wounded for the sake of the crucified have already tasted the coming age of resurrection in which love and justice dawns on us.

---

17. I am not suggesting dealing with these layers as if they were unrelated. However, we can still focus on one layer at a time before relating each of them to a comprehensive perception of the cross.

The cross is also the place where God conquered sin and where his wisdom shines. Indeed, we are the people of the cross, but we are also the people of resurrection.

Discussion Questions

1. In the cross we encounter both the injustice of the world and God's response to that injustice. What are some of the injustices specific to your own social, cultural, and political context? How do you see the cross embodying God's response to those injustices?

2. In being asked to take up our crosses in following Christ, we, too, are being asked to face the world's injustice and respond as followers of Christ. What does that look like in your own specific context? How can you live out what it means to be a "person of the cross" in your day-to-day life?

3. Even as Jesus goes to the cross willingly, he challenges his unjust treatment at the hands of the high priest (John 18:20–23). How can we take up our own crosses as Jesus did – in love and obedience, yet without acquiescing to violence, injustice, and oppression?

4. How does the cross impact your sense of identity – who you are called to be in Christ? In what ways does being a person of the cross require one to also be a person whose identity is rooted in love, the Spirit, the vine, unity, and persecution? To what degree do these identities reinforce each other?

5. In what ways does the cross impact your perspective, not just of your own identity, but of God's? What does the cross communicate to you about God's nature? If, in the cross, we encounter "the crucified God who suffers" – what does that mean to you on a personal level?

16

The People of Resurrection

The fact that Christ appeared to his disciples is the greatest Johannine proof of the resurrection. Most disciples did not believe because they saw an empty grave; no, they believed because they saw the living Christ. John demonstrates the resurrection of Christ through four appearances: (1) to Mary Magdalene, (2) to the disciples without Thomas, (3) to the disciples with Thomas, and (4) to the disciples at the Sea of Galilee. The first three appearances occur in the first week after the resurrection (20:1, 19, 26), and such a week might indeed indicate the beginning of a new age, the age of resurrection. Let us look more closely at these four appearances.

First, Christ appeared to Mary Magdalene. She went to the grave twice and went to the disciples twice. Her first visit to the grave was early in the morning while it was still dark (John 20:1). Graves in ancient, as well as contemporary, Palestinian cultures are repellant places that people avoid. Many still believe that graveyards are places for evil spirits, especially when it is dark. Graveyards in Palestine are also places for thieves, drug addicts, and criminals. The Gospel of Matthew speaks of the demons in the Gadarenes' tombs (Matt 8:24–28), and Mark records the story of a man possessed by an unclean spirit living in the graveyard (Mark 5:2–3). Tombs were unclean places according to the Mosaic law, a place for the residence of unclean spirits.[1] Anyone who touched a dead corpse was defiled (Num 19:11–12). Furthermore, graveyards were not safe. Thieves would go to steal the strips of linen used on the bodies. Grave robbery was common during the time of the early church, prompting Emperor Claudius' decision to execute any grave robber.[2]

In short, Mary was truly brave, for she took the risk of going to a dark, unclean, and dangerous graveyard. She loved Christ, though, and was willing

---

1. Blomberg, *Matthew*, 151.
2. Billington, "Nazareth Inscription."

to risk everything. At the tomb, she discovered that the stone had been rolled away. Confused, she went to Simon Peter and John spreading further confusion through her report. She said, "They have taken the Lord out of the tomb, and we don't know where they have put him!" (John 20:2). Her report does not tell us the identity of the subject of either clause: we don't know who took the Lord, and we also don't know the identity of those who don't know.

Put differently, some unknown people (we) don't know who took the corpse (they) and don't know its current location. Consequently, Peter and John ran to an unclean graveyard. John arrived first, most likely because he was younger than Peter and more physically fit, but the beloved disciple did not enter the tomb. Peter entered and saw the linen strips in place. Thus, there was no robbery. There had to be another explanation. Then John entered the tomb; he saw and believed. This was the first post-resurrection belief in Jesus.

As an aside, we can see, in this narrative, hints of the positive contribution of archaeology in enabling people to believe. This is part of our spirituality in the Holy Land, where the very stones testify to the birth, life, death, and resurrection of our Lord. Jerusalem alone is such a unique place. It is part of our spiritual responsibility not only to maintain biblical sites but also to make sure that their testimony continues to honor our risen Lord. It is the duty of every Christian in Israel and Palestine to take care of these sites.

Returning to Mary, after she shared her first report with John and Peter, she went back to the tomb, crying. She was imprisoned by her grief for Christ. He was the one who fought against oppression, defended the widow, empowered the orphan, and stood with marginalized women. He defended truth, destroying the kingdom of the devil. He was a young man whose youth was stolen by the soldiers of the occupation when the religious leaders decided to kill him. He was a Palestinian Jew who fought against Satan everywhere and who exposed all forms of evil. Like his compatriots, he suffered from political, religious, and social evils. But different from everyone else, he forgave sins, healed the blind, opened the ears of the dumb, and raised the dead.

Nevertheless, like the rest of us, he died. Could it be that evil had the last word? Could it be that oppression won the battle? We know that Mary Magdalene was sad and hopeless. The hope of the whole country was gone. She came to the graveyard, to the land of death and defilement, and imprisoned in grief, her mind was cloudy. Thus, she was not able to perceive the prophecies related to the resurrection of the Christ. Grief blinded her insight and deafened her ears even though it testified to her loyalty to Christ.

Two angels appeared to her in white garments. People were usually terrified when they encountered angels. For example, Daniel was afraid when the angel

Gabriel came to him (Dan 8:16–17), and when Zechariah saw the angel of the Lord on the right side of the altar of incense, he was startled and gripped with fear (Luke 1:11–12). The Blessed Mary was afraid when she saw the angel Gabriel (Luke 1:27–30), and the shepherds were terrified when an angel of the Lord appeared to them (Luke 2:9).

But Mary Magdalene was not afraid; she was overwhelmed with grief. When two angels appeared to her, she continued to cry. The angels spoke to her, but her emotional state was static. When Christ appeared to her it was God himself, but she thought that he was the gardener. Then she accused him of stealing the body and demanded the corpse. She insisted on grieving, on looking for a dead Christ, giving in to a worldview that excluded resurrection. But Christ appeared to her and said, "Mary" (John 20:16). Christ ended her captivity to grief, her enslavement to sorrow and a worldview that lacked resurrection. He did it by calling her name.

Only the good shepherd calls his sheep by name and brings them out to the good pasture (John 10:3). The resurrection of Christ is thus connected to the resurrection of Mary. She rose from the imprisonment of grief and a worldview that limited God. Mary now recognized that Jesus was alive. She wanted to take hold of him, and thus he said to her: "Do not hold on to me, for I have not yet ascended to the Father" (John 20:17). Holding is more than mere touching, so Jesus might be saying to stop hanging on to him. The reason behind Jesus's statement is not ritual cleanness but something related to his ascension. The Bible says, "Do not hold on to me, for I have not yet ascended to the Father" (John 20:17). Mary's relationship to Jesus would be shaped by his ascension to the Father. She could no longer relate to him only from the perspective of the incarnation but must know him through the Spirit.

The age of resurrection had dawned, and new creation was possible because of the work of the Spirit. The Bible says, "Exalted to the right hand of God, he has received from the Father the promised Holy Spirit and has poured out what you now see and hear" (Acts 2:33). The Bible informs us that the age of the Holy Spirit has come, and no one can say that Jesus is Lord except by the Spirit (see 1 Cor 12:3).

Mary returned to the apostles, but with a different message, since Christ had commissioned her to be a messenger of his resurrection. She was his first post-resurrection missionary, amazing in any society dominated by men.[3]

---

3. Even if we don't consider the story of the woman caught in adultery in John 8, there can be no doubt that John is interested in women and the critical roles they play. He spoke about the mother of Jesus at the wedding of Cana (ch. 2), the Samaritan woman (ch. 4), the woman caught in adultery (ch. 8), the sisters of Lazarus (ch. 11), the woman who poured out the perfume

Jesus said to Mary, "I am ascending to my Father and your Father, to my God and your God" (John 20:17). Jesus distinguished his relationship to the Father from the rest of humanity in that he did not use the pronoun "our" and say "our God" and "our Father." We are the children of God by creation just like our father Adam (Luke 3:38). We are also the children of God by adoption through redemption. But Christ, born from the Father before all the ages, is unique in his relationship to the Father. There is no one like him.

Thus, John distinguishes between Christ's sonship and ours, saying, "my Father and your Father." John uses the word "son" to refer to Christ but uses the word "child" to refer to other human beings. The Johannine expression "child" is related to being born, but the expression "son" is connected to a status. We cannot impose Pauline meanings of these expressions on John, and we should respect the unique usage of these expressions in John. Furthermore, John distinguishes between the way the Son relates to God and the rest of humanity relates to God. Jesus says, "My God and your God." The Father is our God. He is our creator and we are the created. His godhood is evident in his nature as well as our created nature. He is eternal, omnipotent, and omniscient; but we are limited by space and time. Our knowledge and ability are limited. The godhood of the Father to the Son is not rooted in a difference in natures but in roles.

The Bible informs us of a godhood that is based on different roles. God told Moses how to relate to his brother Aaron. He said, "You shall speak to him and put words in his mouth; I will help both of you speak and will teach you what to do. He will speak to the people for you, and it will be as if he were your mouth and as if you were God to him" (Exod 4:15–16). The Hebrew text is even stronger than the English translation and says, literally, "You shall be a god to him." The book of Exodus also says, "Then the Lord said to Moses, 'See, I have made you like God to Pharaoh, and your brother Aaron will be your prophet'" (Exod 7:1). Again, the Hebrew text literally reads, "I have made you God to Pharaoh" or "I have made you a god to Pharaoh." How can Moses be a god? In what sense is he a god? It seems that his godhood is conditioned by providing the word of God and representing the God of Israel. The words of God become the words of Moses. Consequently, when someone disobeys Moses, they are disobeying God. The human essence or nature of Moses is not different from Pharaoh or Aaron, but his role is different because God spoke to him. John says, "If he called them 'gods,' to whom the word of God came –

(ch. 12), and Mary (ch. 20). It is indeed important to empower women to serve Christ without any obstacles.

and Scripture cannot be set aside. . . ." (John 10:35). In short, the word "god" means the one who has the power and the highest authority.

Human beings used this word to describe God and his unique nature which is unlike any other being. But we sometimes need to distinguish the theological meaning from the linguistic as well as the literary meanings. For example, when we describe someone as a goddess of beauty, we are not suggesting that people worship her. The context of our words describes her beauty and does not require worship. Context is our guide for perceiving the meaning and nuances of words. The word "god" might be used in reference to human beings, as we have seen in the above discussion, but the context is clear that Moses is not considered God by nature. Instead, he has divine authority in his role as a spokesperson for God.

In summary, the godhood of the Father to the Son is different from his godhood to us. The Father and the Son have the same essence but have different roles. For example, the incarnated Son was crucified, but the Father was not crucified. Christ revealed this reality and his uniqueness to Mary, and then he sent her to declare to the apostles what he had told her. He empowered her to share her experience. She had seen the living Lord, so Mary went back to the apostles, this time with a different message. She was a messenger who was not concerned with a dead corpse but with the living Christ. Her first message caused confusion, but her second message spread life and hope. Mary was now free from her bondage, and with a different message, she had left the circle of death, grief, and lack of understanding to be a messenger of life, joy, and good news. She rose from her death to a glorious life. She became the first missionary for the resurrected Christ and the coming age – an age in which all forms of evil will become extinct. The evil of individuals, as well as all other forms of evil, will end. Political evil, social evil, and the evil of gender discrimination will end. The power of the resurrection that touched Mary impacted her thoughts, feelings, and message.

Perhaps Mary is similar to Palestinians. Palestinians are grieving because they have lost their young men and women. They continually experience political and religious oppression. They frequent graveyards carrying with them the burden of sorrow and despair. Although they live in a circle of hopelessness and death, the one who released Mary from her circle of death can also empower them with his life. Christ can raise Palestine and end all forms of enslavement. He is the way, the truth, and the life. He conquered death and can conquer all forms of sin.

Second, after Mary Magdalene, Christ appeared to the apostles without Thomas on the evening of the first day of his resurrection (John 20:19). Later, he also appeared to Thomas, showing him his hands and side to affirm to everyone that he was not a ghost but the Christ, who rose from the dead with a glorified body. He rose indeed. He was the same person who died; the disciples saw the body that was sown in weakness but now was resurrected in power. Neither Pilate, nor Caiaphas, nor Caesar, nor even death itself was able to conquer Christ or hinder the coming of his kingdom.

Some Jews have asked how the dead will rise. How will God grant us a new body after our death? Shammai and his followers believed the following sequence of events: God would bring the bones, cover them with flesh, then skin, and later he would blow his spirit to give it life.[4] The teachings of Shammai might be congruent with the book of Ezekiel in which God says, "I will attach tendons to you and make flesh come upon you and cover you with skin; I will put breath in you, and you will come to life" (Ezek 37:6). Thus we see that the school of Shammai insisted on connecting the body of resurrection with the body of death.[5] On the other hand, the school of Hillel was closer in its teachings to the book of Job: "Did you not pour me out like milk and curdle me like cheese, clothe me with skin and flesh and knit me together with bones and sinews?" (Job 10:10–11). They saw that bones are provided after flesh and skin.[6] They believed that God would create the resurrection body from nothing and without any connection to the body of death.[7] In short, both schools agreed that a person would be raised from the dead with a body, not only in spirit.

Put differently, the body of the incarnation was the body that dies. Through the resurrection it was transformed into the body that does not die. There are several forms of humanity: the humanity of Adam before falling into sin, his humanity after sinning, the humanity of the incarnation that dies, and the humanity of the resurrection that is superior to all other forms of humanity. The age of the resurrected humanity dawned in the resurrection of Christ. His resurrection indicates a new age for a new humanity. Unlike the sinful humanity of Adam, Christ is a sinless human. Through him, the humanity of death is transformed into the humanity of life. It is the resurrected humanity that conquered all forms of death and extends life to individuals, communities, and the cosmos. More than the immortality of the soul, this resurrection addresses the problem of the destruction of the body and its return to dust. The

---

4. Wright, *Resurrection*, 195.

5. Wright, 196.

6. Wright, 195.

7. Wright, 196.

humanity of Adam becomes the seed that dies and, through the resurrection of Christ, is transformed into a new humanity.

Christ wanted to spread the resurrected humanity. He said, "'Peace be with you! As the Father has sent me, I am sending you.' And with that he breathed on them and said, 'Receive the Holy Spirit'" (John 20:21–22). No doubt the resurrection is connected to the Passover; Christ is the lamb of the Passover. The exodus Passover is a religiopolitical event by which the Jewish people remember being freed from the slavery of Egypt and from political as well as economical oppression. The resurrection has also been connected to the end of exile and the revival of the people of God. Ezekiel 37 uses the language of resurrection to explain the end of exile and the dawn of a new Davidic age.

The language of resurrection is associated with ending the state of death and initiating the state of life – that is, better life. We see this language in the story of the prodigal son who was dead and is now alive (Luke 15:24). Furthermore, the disciples understood that the resurrection of Christ was not only related to one individual but was also connected to the dawning of a new age in which the kingdom of God would spread all over the world. John explains that the transformation of current realities is associated with the activity of the people of resurrection – people who will spread the message of the resurrected Christ and the new humanity. Thus, Jesus blew his spirit and said, "Receive the Holy Spirit," declaring the beginning of the new creation. Just as God blew his spirit into Adam and the latter became a living soul, now Christ was blowing his spirit onto his disciples, transforming them into the new creation. He sent them to the whole earth saying, "As the Father has sent me, I am sending you. . . . If you forgive anyone's sins, their sins are forgiven; if you do not forgive them, they are not forgiven" (John 20:21–23). Christ thus pointed out that the main problem of the first creation was sin and suggested that the main solution was the forgiveness of sin. This forgiveness was founded on his death and resurrection and was to be spread by the empowerment of the Spirit. But we ask, "What is the meaning of forgiveness?"

Several theologians distinguish between vertical and horizontal forgiveness, the forgiveness of God and that of human beings. In the vertical dimension, God forgives the sins of human beings. In the horizontal one, human beings forgive the sins of other human beings. Furthermore, theologians distinguish between saving forgiveness and sanctifying forgiveness. The first was accomplished on the cross, and we receive it by grace through faith. The second kind of forgiveness, sanctifying forgiveness, is needed every day.[8] The one who sins

---

8. For further information, see Nelson, "Exegeting Forgiveness," 33–34.

becomes indebted to the person he or she has sinned against and must either pay his debt or receive free forgiveness from that person.

There are two schools of thought in addressing the horizontal aspect of forgiveness: conditional and unconditional forgiveness. The first makes repentance a condition for forgiveness, arguing that the horizontal form of forgiveness must be like the vertical form.[9] That is, a person who does not repent will not be saved and will suffer the consequences of his or her sin. The vertical and horizontal forms of forgiveness are clearly related in the writings of Paul, who said, "Be kind and compassionate to one another, forgiving each other, just as in Christ God forgave you" (Eph 4:32). Furthermore, Christ said, "If your brother or sister sins against you, rebuke them; and if they repent, forgive them" (Luke 17:3). On the other hand, those who advocate unconditional forgiveness argue that Christ forgave unconditionally.[10] When he was on the cross, he said, "Father, forgive them, for they do not know what they are doing" (Luke 23:34). Stephen followed in the same footsteps of Jesus when he prayed for his killers and said: "Lord, do not hold this sin against them" (Acts 7:60).

Regardless of our position concerning conditional or unconditional forgiveness, we should pay attention to the following:[11] (1) Forgiveness is different from reconciliation. When relationships are broken it is not enough to forgive; we also need to pursue reconciliation as ambassadors of Christ. Reconciliation requires building bridges of trust, pure Christian love, and uncompromising truth. We should address all forms of evil just as Christ did. We should not stop with horizontal forgiveness and ignore our responsibility towards the oppressed as well as the oppressors. (2) Forgiveness does not mean declaring the guilty innocent or softening the ugliness of his or her guilt. It does not mean overlooking the standards of justice that God has established in the state (Rom 13:1–7), the church (1 Cor 6:1–11), the family (Eph 6:1–4), and the Holy Scriptures. Therefore, judges condemn evildoers even if they repent; churches establish judges; families discipline their children. Despite the forgiveness of Jesus and Stephen, unrepentant evildoers are still responsible

---

9. Wolterstorff, "What Makes Forgiveness Possible"; Caneday, *Must Christians Always Forgive?*, 10.

10. MacArthur, *Freedom and Power*, 122.

11. It seems to me that unconditional forgiveness is closer to a biblical worldview. Nevertheless, this is not the right place to provide a detailed argument. It is also important to point out that the school of unconditional forgiveness errs when it marginalizes the importance of justice and reconciliation. We also need to distinguish between God's personal act of forgiveness and legal acts of forgiveness. The forgiveness of Christ on the cross does not annul divine judgment and human responsibility before the divine court.

before divine judgment. (3) God has called us to love all people whether they are repentant or unrepentant. We must speak from the logic of love and be clothed with love in our actions and feelings. We must be motivated by love and be patient, merciful, and hopeful. There is no place for apathy, bitterness, holding grudges, gossip, or revenge.

When a person forgives, they must admit that something wrong happened or there was an offense. After considering the offensive action or attitude, the Christian offers forgiveness. This forgiveness is offered because of the spilled blood of the Son of God on the cross. The foundation of Christian horizontal forgiveness is the vertical forgiveness revealed on the cross. There is no forgiveness without guilt. We forgive the guilty, not the innocent. We forgive sinners, not the righteous.[12] Reconciliation does not occur by ignoring justice, guilt, or repentance. The guilty party must confess his sin and repent in order to move towards reconciliation. Forgiveness is the first step to address evil from the perspective of love. But it is not the last.

Stopping at the first step is not only contrary to the wisdom of God, but it also causes the spread of evil as well as the marginalizing of justice. We should not downplay the ugliness of evil or give excuses to those who practice it. Forgiveness does not require softening our view of oppression or evil, downplaying its destructive implications, hiding the pain caused by sinful actions, or forgetting what has been done. It does, however, require our refusal to respond to the guilty party with revenge or in evil ways. Instead, we choose to respond in biblical love. We condemn the evil but continue to bless the evildoer.

Thus, forgiveness is missional. It connects horizontal forgiveness with the vertical. We become messengers in the world by spreading vertical forgiveness. The forgiver goes to the recipient of forgiveness. It is the responsibility of the forgiver to reveal the evil and the solution that God offers. The forgiver is a messenger of justice and biblical love. Otherwise, the act of forgiveness lacks the understanding of God's will. If the guilty party responds positively and repents then the two sides can move forward towards reconciliation.

Furthermore, if someone sins against you and you go to them, but they neither listen nor repent, then we have to address evil differently. Matthew says, "If your brother or sister sins, go and point out their fault, just between the two of you. If they listen to you, you have won them over" (Matt 18:15). But what shall we do if they don't listen? Matthew adds, "But if they will not listen, take one or two others along. . . . If they still refuse to listen, tell it to

---

12. Wolterstorff, "What Makes Forgiveness Possible."

the church; and if they refuse to listen even to the church, treat them as you would a pagan or a tax collector" (Matt 18:16–17). Put differently, we should pursue full reconciliation, not only forgiveness. The way of reconciliation is not only the path of love but is also the path of repentance, justice, and communal transformation. The whole community is impacted by a single act of injustice.

Third, after appearing to the disciples, Jesus appeared to Thomas. Thomas refused to accept the disciples' report about the resurrection of Christ (John 20:25). He did not understand the Old Testament writings concerning Christ (we know from the story of the two Emmaus disciples that Moses and the prophets speak of the Christ [Luke 24:13–49]), but Thomas also did not understand the teachings of Christ concerning himself – his death and resurrection. He neither accepted the testimony of Mary Magdalene, nor did he endorse the interpretation of John, who believed when he saw the empty grave. He did not accept the report of the apostles when they said, "We have seen the Lord." Instead, he rejected all these testimonies and prophecies, setting up his own standards for correct decisions. He did not reflect on the possibility that Christ had heard all of his statements.

Jesus, though, decided to encounter Thomas in person at the beginning of the week. He appeared to his doubting follower and showed him his wounded hands and pierced side in order to encourage him to walk in the way of faith. The people of resurrection are a community who believe in the living Christ. Consequently, Thomas said, "My Lord and My God." The literal translation is: "You are the Lord to me, and you are the God to me." The Greek text uses *ho theos*. The presence of the article (*ho*) before the divine name challenges Jehovah's Witnesses who claim that this article is used only to denote God with a big G. In their perspective, the divinity of Christ is less than the divinity of the Father. *Ho theos* in their mistaken worldview is reserved for the full divinity of the Father. Jehovah's Witnesses claim that Jesus is a god and not God, basing their conclusion upon several arguments that include the absence of the definite article before the Greek word *theos*, especially in John 1:1. Their interpretation ignores the proper understanding of Greek grammar, the Johannine context, and even the context of the whole New Testament which was written by people who believed in one God. The word *theos* without the definite article appears 282 times in the New Testament to denote the one God.

This is a stark challenge to the teachings of Jehovah's Witnesses. For example, John uses the word *theos* without the definite article in John 1:12, 13, and 18. Without doubt, John believes in the full divinity of Christ in the introduction of his book, as well as throughout its pages. Now, he writes the words of Thomas: "You are my Lord and my God." When Christ heard Thomas's declaration of worship, he did not rebuke him but accepted his statements and affirmed the importance of faith, especially for those who don't see.

Fourth, after Thomas, Christ appeared to the disciples at the Sea of Galilee. He was interested in restoring a right relationship with his followers, and, while the previous meeting had been for Thomas, this meeting was dedicated to restoring Peter. Peter had denied Christ. In doing so, he denied his own identity and calling, but he wept bitterly, expressing not only his regret but also his repentance. He also returned and stayed with the rest of the disciples.

Christ prepared a fire not unlike the fire around which Peter had stood on the night of his betrayal. Coal is mentioned twice: once in the context of denial and the other in the context of reconciliation (18:18; 21:9). Christ appeared to Peter and the disciples and prepared a meal for them. After they ate and were satisfied, Christ spoke to Peter saying, "Simon son of John, do you love me more than these?" (21:15). Jesus repeated the question three times in different ways. The use of synonyms is not particularly significant in the Gospel of John. Indeed, John uses more than one word to express the idea of love, but the context decides the meaning, not the definition of the word. The idea that certain words denote divine love, while others denote friendship, is not accurate and contradicts how John uses these pertinent words.

In any case, Peter was sad because Christ asked him three times, reminding him of his three denials. Christ not only forgave Peter; he also sought reconciliation. He wanted to rebuild trust with Peter and to commission him to take care of his sheep, saying, "Take care of my sheep" (21:16). Thus, Christ asserts that the sheep belong to Christ, not to Peter. The motive for taking care of the sheep is love of Christ, not the loveliness of the sheep. When Peter obeys Christ out of love for him, then he will be able to fulfill his mission. Taking care of the sheep is not a job or a profession but a divine mission that depends on divine calling. Love is the way to discover this calling. Peter, through loving Christ, discovered his calling as a shepherd.

Discussion Questions

1. In this chapter, Mary Magdalene is compared to the Palestinian people, burdened under the weight of their sorrow and despair. What corporate griefs – on the national or ethnic level – are being carried by the members of your community?

2. How might God be desiring to enact resurrection, on a communal and not just a personal level, in your community? How might the church partner with this work of resurrection?

3. Mary Magdalene was resurrected from her imprisonment to grief – her hopelessness. What resurrections has God enacted in your own life?

4. Do you see your calling to forgive as a missional calling? As something that testifies to the problem of sin and the forgiveness of God? Can you pinpoint times in your life when God has used forgiveness to witness to those around you? Or, perhaps, when God has used forgiveness to witness to *you*?

5. Do you believe that horizontal forgiveness should be unconditional or conditional? Why?

Conclusion

This book has argued that the Gospel of John presents a new world order in which the major components of Pharisaic Judaism are deconstructed and then reconstructed in relation to the centrality of the inclusive Christ. It has also pointed out the contextual implications of John's arguments in Israel/Palestine. The following are some salient points that we should highlight.

First, both Palestinians and Jews should avoid the temptation of employing the identity of Christ to make political gains. Christ is fully human and can represent both Palestinians and Jews. We cannot and should not understand the identity of Christ in an ethnically exclusive way. The Chalcedonian Christ is fully human and is inclusive. He does not exclude any nation. It is important for us to understand the nature of the Christ that we follow. He is not the Christ who rejects Palestinians or Jews or any other person. He is not the Christ who pushes people away, refusing to engage them, because God loves all nations. Every human being is created in the image of God. Therefore, we should respect everyone without exception. In fact, every human being is a gift from God. The value of human beings is not only related to our creation in the image of God but also to the incarnation in which humanity has been honored and elevated.[1] Humanity has also been elevated in the resurrection of Christ. Through Christ, the fallen created being has been transformed into a glorified being. It is clear that Christ was born in a Jewish culture, but his human identity has redefined Jewishness in inclusive ways. Put differently, through Christ historical Jewishness has been reread in light of eschatological Jewishness. Christ is not only a historical Jew, he is also an eschatological Jew. Greater than any other Jew, he redefines Judaism in inclusive ways and has embodied its deepest hopes. He is fully human and can represent all human beings.

Second, our understanding of holy space and the promise of the land should not be divorced from the centrality of Christ as well as a worldview that highlights this centrality. Any trustworthy Christian interpretation of the Old Testament should take into consideration how John – and perhaps the rest of the New Testament – has reread the Old Testament in light of the coming of Christ. Furthermore, our understanding of the temple, the Sabbath, the exodus tradition, the wilderness traditions, the children of Abraham, the

---

1. Khoury, (خوري).من أجل حدود مفتوحة بين الزمن والأبدية: الحضور المسيحي [For an open border between time and eternity: The Christian presence], 145.

holy land, and life itself should be shaped by the centrality of Jesus Christ. This centrality defines faith as well as hermeneutics – how we are to read and interpret Scripture. Since Christ is fully human, both Palestinians and Jews can see him as their hero and savior.

Stated a bit differently, we have discussed the inclusive Johannine Christ in this book. First, we discussed rereading Pharisaic Judaism in light of the coming of Christ. John has presented a new world order based on the centrality of Christ and his inclusive identity and vision. Christ is the groom of the messianic age. He is the temple and the Sabbath. He is the center of holy history, holy people, holy land, and even life itself. We have explained that, from John's perspective, a right reading of the Old Testament is connected to Christ. Then, we pointed out seven aspects of the identity of the people of God in the book of the hour. They are the people of love, the people of the Spirit, the persecuted people, the people of the vine, the people of unity, the people of the cross, and the people of resurrection. All these identities are missional. We have elaborated on each one of these identities, not only as seen in John but also from a contextual Palestinian point of view.

Finally, I pray that all readers will find this book helpful. All Glory to God.

Bibliography

Abdel Salam, Farouk (فاروق عبد السلام). محمد في إنجيل يوحنا [Muhammad in the Gospel of John]. Cairo: Mrkz Aslsam Lltjhyz Alfny.

Abu Shawar, Saadi (سعدي أبو شاور). تطوّر الإتجاه الوطنيّ في الشِّعر الفلسطيني المعاصر [The evolution of the national trend in contemporary Palestinian poetry]. Beirut: Alm'essh Al'erbyh Lldrasat Walnshr, 2003.

Alighieri, Dante (دانتي أليجييري). الكوميديا الإلهية [The divine comedy]. Cairo: Dar Alm'earf, 1955.

Ateek, Naim. *Justice and Only Justice: A Palestinian Theology of Liberation*. Maryknoll: Orbis, 1989.

———. *A Palestinian Christian Cry for Reconciliation*. Maryknoll: Orbis, 2008.

Beasley-Murray, George R. *John*. Vol. 36 of Word Biblical Commentary. Dallas: Word, 2002.

Billington, Clyde. "The Nazareth Inscription: Proof of the Resurrection of Christ?" Associates for Biblical Research. July 2009. https://biblearchaeology.org/research/new-testament-era/2857-the-nazareth-inscription-proof-of-the-resurrection-of-christ-part-i.

Blomberg, C. *Matthew*. Nashville: Broadman & Holman, 1992.

Borgen, Peder. "Logos Was the True Light: Contributions to the Interpretation of the Prologue of John." *Novum Testamentum* 14 (1972): 115–130.

Brand, Chad, ed. *Perspectives on Israel and the Church: Four Views*. Nashville: Broadman & Holman, 2015.

Brodie, Thomas. *The Gospel According to John: A Literary and Theological Commentary*. Oxford: Oxford University Press, 1993.

Brown, Jeannine. "Creation's Renewal in the Gospel of John." *Catholic Biblical Quarterly* 72 (2010): 275–290.

Brown, Raymond, and Francis Moloney. *An Introduction to the Gospel of John*. New York: Doubleday, 2003.

Brueggemann, Walter. *Sabbath as Resistance: Saying No to the Culture of Now*. Louisville: Westminster John Knox, 2014.

Bulembat, Jean-Bosco. "Head-Waiter and Bridegroom of the Wedding of Cana." *Journal for the Study of the New Testament* 30 (2007): 55–73.

Busters, Cyril (كيرلس بسترس). مدخل إلى اللاهوت الأدبي [Introduction to literary theology]. Jwnyh: Mnshwrat Almktbh Albwlsyh, 1995.

Caneday, Ardel. *Must Christians Always Forgive?* Mount Hermon: Center for Cultural Leadership, 2011.

Carson, D. A. *The Gospel According to John*. Grand Rapids: Eerdmans, 1991.

Chafer, Lewis. *Systematic Theology*. Vol. 7. Dallas: Dallas Seminary Press, 1948.

Crutcher, Rhonda. *That He Might Be Revealed*. Eugene: Pickwick, 2015.

Danesi, Marcel. *The Semiotics of Love*. Cham, Switzerland: Palgrave Macmillan, 2019.

Davis, Anne. "Israel's Inheritance: Birthright of the First Born." *Chafer Seminary Journal* 13 (2008): 79–94.

Derrett, J. Duncan. *Law in the New Testament*. Eugene: Wipf & Stock, 1970.

Dillow, Joseph. "Abiding Is Remaining in Fellowship: Another Look at John 15:1–16." *Bibliotheca Sacra* 147, no. 585 (1990): 44–53.

Dodd, C. H. *The Interpretation of the Fourth Gospel*. Cambridge: Cambridge University Press, 1953.

Easley, Kendell. "Prayer Customs in First Century Judaism." *Biblical Illustrator* (1996): 48–50.

El Meskeen, Matta (متى المسكين).(الإنجيل بحسب القديس يوحنا: دراسة وتفسير وشرح [The Gospel According to St John: Study, interpretation, and explanation]. Cairo: Dyr Alqdys Anba Mqar, 1990.

Elowsky, Joel, ed. *Commentary on John: Cyril of Alexandria Volume 1*. Downers Grove: InterVarsity Press, 2013.

———, ed. *Commentary on John: Cyril of Alexandria Volume 2*. Downers Grove: InterVarsity Press, 2015.

———, ed. *Commentary on the Gospel of John: Theodore of Mopsuestia*. Downers Grove: InterVarsity Press, 2010.

El Sakka, Ahmed [أحمد السقا]. بيركليت [Berkelet]. Cairo: Mktbh Almty'ey, 1972.

Enz, Jacob. "The Book of Exodus as a Literary Type for the Gospel of John." *Journal of Biblical Literature* 76 (1957): 208–215.

Harrison, R. K. "Feasts and Festivals of Israel." In *Baker Encyclopedia of the Bible Vol. 1*, edited by Walter A. Elwell, 783–788. Grand Rapids: Baker, 1988.

Harvey, Richard. *Mapping Messianic Jewish Theology*. Milton Keynes: Paternoster, 2009.

Hayden, Neb. *When the Good News Gets Even Better: Rediscovering the Gospels through First-Century Jewish Eyes*. Colorado Springs: David Cook, 2009.

Hengel, Martin. *Crucifixion: In the Ancient World and the Folly of the Message of the Cross*. Philadelphia: Fortress Press, 1977.

———. *The Helenization of Judaea in the First Century after Christ*. Philadelphia: Trinity Press International, 1989.

Hoekema, Anthony. *The Bible and the Future*. Grand Rapids: Eerdmans, 1994.

Hoskins, Paul. "Freedom from Slavery to Sin and the Devil: John 8:31–47 and the Passover Theme of the Gospel of John." *Trinity Journal* 31 (2010): 47–63.

———. *Jesus as the Fulfillment of the Temple in the Gospel of John*. Milton Keynes: Paternoster, 2007.

Inbari, Motti. *Jewish Fundamentalism and the Temple Mount: Who Will Build the Third Temple?* Albany: State University of New York Press, 2009.

Joines, Karen. "The Bronze Serpent in the Israelite Cult." *Journal of Biblical Literature* 87 (1968): 245–256.

Josephus, Flavius. *The Antiquities of the Jews*. Translated by William Whiston. Project Gutenberg, 4 January 2009. Updated 9 August 2017. https://www.gutenberg.org/files/2848/2848-h/2848-h.htm.

———. *The Wars of the Jews*. Translated by William Whiston. Project Gutenberg, 10 January 2009. Updated 3 August 2013. https://www.gutenberg.org/files/2850/2850-h/2850-h.htm.

Katanacho, Yohanna (حنا كتناشو). فمن أنت؟... أنا هو [I Am . . . Who are you?]. 2nd ed. Jerusalem: Christian and Missionary Alliance, 2008.

———. "Palestinian Protestant Theological Responses to a World Marked by Violence." *Missiology: An International Review* 36 (2008): 289–305.

———. "Reading the Gospel of John through Palestinian Eyes." In *Jesus without Borders: Christology in Global Context*, edited by Gene Green, Stephen Pardue, and K. K. Yeo, 103–122. Carlisle, UK: Langham Global Library, 2014.

———. Review of *Perspectives on Israel and the Church: Four Views*, edited by Chad Brand. *Themelios* 41 (2016): 153–155.

Katanacho, Yohanna, and Dina Katanacho (حنا ودينا كتناشو). أطلقوني [Free me]. Jerusalem: Knysh Alathad Almsyhy, 2002.

Khoury, Rafiq (رفيق خوري).بين الحضور المسيحي في المشرق العربي من أجل حدود مفتوحة بين الزمن والأبدية: الماضي والحاضر والمستقبل [For an open border between time and eternity: The Christian presence in the Arab East between the past, present and future]. Bethlehem: Mrkz Allqaʾ, 2014.

———. من أجل حدود مفتوحة بين الزمن والأبدية: نحو لاهوت متجسد في تربة بلادنا. [For an open border between time and eternity: Towards theology embodied in the soil of our country]. Bethlehem: Mrkz Allqaʾ, 2012.

Kim, Stephen. "The Relationship of John 1:19–51 to the Book of Signs in John 2–12." *Bibliotheca Sacra* 165 (2008): 323–337.

Kjaer-Hansen, Kai. "An Introduction to the Names Yehoshua/Joshua, Yeshua, Jesus and Yeshu." JewsforJesus.org (1992): https://jewsforjesus.org/answers/an-introduction-to-the-names-yehoshua/joshua-yeshua-jesus-and-yeshu/.

Kostenberger, Andreas. "Jesus the Good Shepherd Who Will Also Bring Other Sheep (John 10:16): The Old Testament Background of a Familiar Metaphor." *Bulletin of Biblical Research* 12 (2002): 67–96.

———. *John*. Grand Rapids: Baker Academic, 2004.

Kysar, Robert. "The Gospel of John in Current Research." *Religious Studies Review* 9 (1983): 314–323.

Laney, Carl. "Abiding Is Believing: The Analogy of the Vine in John 15: 1–6." *Bibliotheca Sacra* 146 (1989): 55–66.

Lewis, Karoline. "Preaching John 8:31–36." *Word and World* 36 (2016): 177–185.

Lincoln, Andrew. *The Gospel According to Saint John*. Peabody: Hendrickson, 2005.

Lizorkin-Eyzenberg, Eli. *The Jewish Gospel of John*. Tel Aviv: Lizorkin-Eyzenberg, 2015.

Lorimer, John (جون لوريمر). تاريخ الكنيسة: الجزء الثالث [Church history: Part three]. Cairo: Dar Althqafh, 1988.

MacArthur, John. *The Freedom and Power of Forgiveness*. Wheaton: Crossway Books, 1998.

Malatesta, Edward. "The Literary Structure of John 17." *Biblica* 52, no. 2 (1971): 190–214.

Martin, James. "John 10:1–10." *Interpretation* 32 (1978): 171–175.

Moltmann, Jurgen. *The Crucified God*. Kindle Edition. London: SCM, 2001.

Moulder, James. "Is a Chalcedonian Christology Coherent?" *Modern Theology* 2 (1986): 285–307.

Nelson, Randy. "Exegeting Forgiveness." *American Theological Inquiry* 5 (2012): 33–58.

Nestle-Aland, *Novum Testamentum Graece*. 28th rev. ed. Stuttgart: Deutsche Bibelgesellschaft, 2015.

Nestlehutt, Mark. "Chalcedonian Christology: Modern Criticism and Contemporary Ecumenism." *Journal of Ecumenical Studies* 35 (1998): 175–196.

Neusner, Jacob. *From Politics to Piety: The Emergence of Pharisaic Judaism*. Eugene: Wipf & Stock, 2003.

Ng, Wai-Yee. *Water Symbolism in John: An Eschatological Interpretation*. New York: Peter Lang, 2001.

Pack, Frank. "The Gospel of John in the Twentieth Century." *Restoration Quarterly* 7 (1963): 173–185.

Pazdan, Mary. "Nicodemus and the Samaritan Woman: Contrasting Models of Discipleship." *Biblical Theology Bulletin* 17 (1987): 145–148.

Perkin, Hazel. "Marriage, Marriage Customs." *Baker Encyclopedia of the Bible Vol. 2*, edited by Walter A. Elwell, 1405–1410. Grand Rapids: Baker, 1988.

Porter, Stanley, and Ron Fay. *The Gospel of John in Modern Interpretations*. Grand Rapids: Kregel, 2018.

Raheb, Mitri. *Faith in the Face of Empire: The Bible through Palestinian Eyes*. Maryknoll: Orbit Books, 2014.

———. *I Am a Palestinian Christian*. Minneapolis: Fortress, 1995.

———. "Toward a Hermeneutics of Liberation: A Palestinian Christian Perspective." In *The Biblical Text in the Context of Occupation: Towards a New Hermeneutics of Liberation*, edited by Mitri Raheb, 11–27. Bethlehem: Diyar, 2012.

Raheb, Mitri, and Suzanne Henderson. *The Cross in Contexts: Suffering and Redemption in Palestine*. Maryknoll: Orbis, 2017. Kindle.

Reinhartz, Adele. *Befriending the Beloved Disciple: A Jewish Reading of the Gospel of John*. New York: Continuum, 2001.

———. "A Nice Jewish Girl Reads the Gospel of John." *Semeia* 77 (1997): 177–193.

Rodkinson, Michael, ed. *Babylonian Talmud*. Boston: Talmud Society, 1918. Available from: archive.org/stream/FullTalmud/FullTalmud_djvu.txt.

Rushton, Kathleen. "The Cosmology of John 1:1–14 and Its Implications for Ethical Action in This Ecological Age." *Colloquium* 45 (2013): 137–153.

Rutledge, Fleming. *The Crucifixion: Understanding the Death of Jesus Christ*. Grand Rapids: Eerdmans, 2015.

Scouteris, Constantine. "The People of God – Its Unity and Its Glory." *Greek Orthodox Theological Review* 30 (1985): 399–420.

Songer, Harold. "The Gospel of John in Recent Research." *Review and Expositor* 62 (1965): 417–428.

Spence-Jones, H. D. M. *The Pulpit Commentary: St John.* New York: Funk & Wagnalls, 2004.

Stibbe, Mark. *The Gospel of John as Literature: An Anthology of Twentieth-Century Perspectives.* Leiden: Brill, 1993.

Stott, John. *The Cross of Christ.* Leicester, UK: Inter-Varsity Press, 1986.

Strange, James. "Nazareth." In *Anchor Bible Dictionary K–N, Vol. 4*, edited by David Noel Freedman, 1050. New York: Doubleday, 1992.

Suggit, John. "Jesus the Gardner: The Atonement in the Fourth Gospel as Re-creation." *Neot* 33, no. 1 (1999): 161–168.

Towner, W. Sibley. "Wedding." In *Harper's Bible Dictionary*, edited by Paul Achtemeir, 1125–1126. New York: HarperCollins, 1996.

Wolterstorff, Nicholas. "What Makes Forgiveness Possible after Injustice." *The Christian Century* 130 (2013): 26–29.

Wright, Christopher. *The Message of Ezekiel.* Downers Grove: InterVarsity Press, 2001.

Wright, David. "Feasts, Festivals, and Fasts." In *Harper's Bible Dictionary*, edited by Paul Achetemeier, 305–307. New York: HarperCollins, 1996.

Wright, N. T. *Jesus and the Victory of God.* Minneapolis: Fortress, 1996.

———. *The Resurrection of the Son of God.* London: Fortress Press, 2003.

Yakan, Amir (أمير يكن). محمد رسول الله في كتابات القديس يوحنا [Muhammed is the messenger of God in the writings of St John]. Damascus: Mktbh Alasd, 1999.

Young, Frances. "The Council of Chalcedon 1550 Years Later." *Touchstone* 19 (2001): 5–14.

Zahran, Muhammad (محمد زهران). إنجيل يوحنا في الميزان [The Gospel of John in scales]. Alzqazyq: Dar Alarqm, 1991.

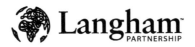

Langham Literature and its imprints are a ministry of Langham Partnership.

Langham Partnership is a global fellowship working in pursuit of the vision God entrusted to its founder John Stott –

> *to facilitate the growth of the church in maturity and Christ-likeness through raising the standards of biblical preaching and teaching.*

Our vision is to see churches in the majority world equipped for mission and growing to maturity in Christ through the ministry of pastors and leaders who believe, teach and live by the Word of God.

Our mission is to strengthen the ministry of the Word of God through:

- nurturing national movements for biblical preaching
- fostering the creation and distribution of evangelical literature
- enhancing evangelical theological education

especially in countries where churches are under-resourced.

Our ministry

Langham Preaching partners with national leaders to nurture indigenous biblical preaching movements for pastors and lay preachers all around the world. With the support of a team of trainers from many countries, a multi-level programme of seminars provides practical training, and is followed by a programme for training local facilitators. Local preachers' groups and national and regional networks ensure continuity and ongoing development, seeking to build vigorous movements committed to Bible exposition.

Langham Literature provides majority world preachers, scholars and seminary libraries with evangelical books and electronic resources through publishing and distribution, grants and discounts. The programme also fosters the creation of indigenous evangelical books in many languages, through writer's grants, strengthening local evangelical publishing houses, and investment in major regional literature projects, such as one volume Bible commentaries like *The Africa Bible Commentary* and *The South Asia Bible Commentary*.

Langham Scholars provides financial support for evangelical doctoral students from the majority world so that, when they return home, they may train pastors and other Christian leaders with sound, biblical and theological teaching. This programme equips those who equip others. Langham Scholars also works in partnership with majority world seminaries in strengthening evangelical theological education. A growing number of Langham Scholars study in high quality doctoral programmes in the majority world itself. As well as teaching the next generation of pastors, graduated Langham Scholars exercise significant influence through their writing and leadership.

To learn more about Langham Partnership and the work we do visit **langham.org**

Milton Keynes UK
Ingram Content Group UK Ltd.
UKHW021026110624
444053UK00014B/819